The Abbe Michonneau found himself in the suburbs of Paris with a working class population largely indifferent or openly antagonistic to the Church. He decided to treat the parish as embracing not merely his good church-goers, but *all* these people. It was to be a missionary parish and his aim was to make all those within his his territory into a true Christian community.

Father Chery, O.P., persuaded the author to tell him how he set about the task, and this book is the result of their conversations. Although this revolution was set in motion some years before the great Encyclical *Mediator Dei* on the liturgy appeared, the Abbe had begun in action a great deal of what the Pope set forth in doctrine. A liturgical parish inspired by true Catholic Action, it will be an inspiration to English speaking priests and laity alike.

Archbishop Cushing of Boston adds his recommendation of the English translation to Cardinal Suhard's long introduction.

REVOLUTION
IN A CITY PARISH

REVOLUTION
IN A
CITY PARISH

BY
ABBÉ MICHONNEAU

WITH A FOREWORD
BY
ARCHBISHOP CUSHING
OF BOSTON

The Newman Press
Westminster, Maryland

1950

First Published in English, 1949

Manufactured by
Universal Lithographers, Inc.
Baltimore 2, Md.
U. S. A.

CONTENTS

Nihil obstat :   Ricardus Roche, S.T.D.,
                   Censor deputatus.

Imprimatur :   ✠ Joseph,
                   Archiepiscopus Birmingamiensis.

Birmingamiae, die 4a Octobris 1948.

FOREWORD

by

His Excellency, the Most Reverend Richard J. Cushing,.
Archbishop of Boston.

Cardinal Suhard of Paris gives warm and unqualified praise to this book of Father Michonneau's. His Eminence describes the work as the outgrowth of practical experience, priestly zeal, and a genuine thirst for souls. It is revolutionary in a sense of that word without sinister connotation. It is a sincere effort to point the way for the renewal of Christianity among the dechristianized proletariat of France.

Thoughtful men in many parts of the world can discover in Father Michonneau's work a pattern for advancing the boundaries of the living Church everywhere, by the use of established Catholic parishes as active cells for such growth.

Father Michonneau notes that, traditionally, the parish has been the expression of religious community life. In the *parish* as it developed in Catholic Europe, practically all human beings dwelling within its confines were, by that very fact, its members. Some individuals were less faithful to their duties than others, but no man, woman or child denied his or her allegiance to the particular unit-cell of the Mystical Body, the parish, within whose confines he or she dwelt.

To-day in France, the author explains, things have become very different. New factors have introduced great changes. In many parts of France there are great masses of humanity who are spiritual drifters. A small number are aggressively irreligious, hostile to their nation's Christian tradition, not merely ignorant but malignantly misinformed on things Christian, bitter in their disdain for the priest and the institution for which he stands. The great majority, however, are merely religion-less; they are not *hostile*, but are completely *ignorant* of Christian life and teaching, unacquainted even with the inside of a house of God.

With France's insufficient clergy, it is hopeless to seek to retrieve the lost ground by operating the parishes as in the days of faith. Instead, this unit of Catholic organization has come, in many cases, to be an outpost for spiritual reconquest. The pastor must now make of himself a captain at the head of loyal lieutenants who are his curates—if he is so fortunate as to have such. His spiritual fighting force, in any case, must more and more include lay apostles, who recognize that Christ can be served best by bringing him into the homes and hearts of every creature of God within the parish confines.

Father Michonneau notes that the 'missionaries' of France must start anew to awaken a consciousness of what Christ means. Their task is quite different from, and even more difficult than that of apostles in China or Japan who announce the Christian message for the first time. In France the populace *thinks* that it knows Christianity; people have long ago dismissed it once and for all as having no practical bearing on their lives or their needs. Christian truths, ideals of Christian beauty, when presented in routine fashion, have no power to 'startle' such people. 'Yes, yes, we've heard all that', they mumble with a shrug, even as they continue their search for values elsewhere. The apostles of modern France must be sufficiently alert and dynamic to persuade these people that they are mistaken—that the quest of man leads to the Christ of the Tabernacle.

We might well apply the findings of Father Michonneau to our English-speaking world. Catholic parish life, it is true, is strong in many parts of England and the United States. But all too often our parishes are far from possessing the truly Catholic concept of the term as it was used in the Middle Ages. Indeed the element of all-embracingness has long since been forgotten. In the Protestant world of to-day the term 'parish' signifies much the same to the Catholic as it does to the Baptist or Methodist. The parish is a sort of spiritual club, the membership of which is composed of chosen adherents within a given area, who live their lives together and ignore all the other inhabitants of the area.

We ask the ordinary Catholic in the English-speaking world: 'How many souls are there in your parish?' He replies immediately with a figure—eight hundred, fifteen hundred, five thousand, ten thousand. And by that figure he means the Catholics alone who dwell within the parish lines. He may say that there are fifteen hundred in his parish, while in point of fact twenty thousand souls may be serving out their lives within its confines. The sense of the authentic Catholic tradition that would embrace the remaining eighteen thousand five hundred has been lost.

And so perhaps we have a lesson for our English-speaking world to learn from Father Michonneau's book on France. Perhaps our parishes must become outposts of spiritual attack. It may be time for each pastor and his curates, even with us, to organize the stronger elements among the laity for an advance that would bring the forgotten and disdained Christ of the Tabernacle not merely to those few who already find their way into our churches, but to the huge multitudes who are outside the Church—but within the parish.

Christ came for all, Christ died for all, Christ calls all, not only the practising Catholic, not only the pagan in China to whom we send our missionaries. He desires as well the millions by our side, the dwellers in our established parishes whom we have accustomed ourselves to overlook. Here is the oldest and yet the newest of apostolates—that to our immediate neighbours. God prosper it!

RICHARD J. CUSHING.

PREFACE TO THE FRENCH EDITION

By His Eminence CARDINAL SUHARD,
Archbishop of Paris.

It is always a happy experience for the shepherd of a diocese to read a record of priestly effort for the conquest of souls, and to see proposed an apostolic way of life which is adapted to the needs of a world that presents a problem of ever-increasing urgency to the Catholic apostolate. I cannot adequately express my thanks to Father Michonneau, and to Father Chéry, his editor, for their portrayal of the parish activity accomplished by a priestly unit at Sacré Coeur de Colombes for the past five years or more. Truly this is an account which should renew and guide the apostolic zeal of those whose mission it is to lead our people on the search for a life that is completely Christian and also compatible with the actual conditions around them.

This book is indeed timely. For years zealous priests have been meditating on the grave words of Pope Pius XI, who said that the scandal of the nineteenth century had been the loss of the working class by the Church. For years now this meditation has been bearing fruit in a large number of activities to which the whole Christian community owes in great part the renewal of its vitality. And these activities, by their very success, call for a deeper enquiry into the problem of winning the common man for Christ. The religious effort itself of the last twenty years in France has raised the questions to which Father Michonneau's labours give a direct answer.

It would be a mistake to think that this volume is concerned only with finding a new clerical technique. Father Michonneau's last wish is to be an instigator of rash changes; he wants, rather, to face squarely the problem of bringing the Gospel into the lives of our people. His constant concern is to find more effective ways of rechristianizing people, and especially the working class of our cities. Everywhere groups of active young working-class Christians have been formed, and these Christians, as they grow up, are going to found an ever-increasing number of Christian homes, which will often be admirable centres of faith and devotion. In the degree, however, that Catholic Action bears fruit, it becomes increasingly clear that a somewhat different task must be undertaken—not opposed to Catholic Action, but complementing it.

We can no longer ignore the fact that these new Christians, born of Catholic Action, must face a world which is practically pagan, one in which there is almost nothing truly Christian. We cannot conceive of a spirituality abstracted from the contacts and influences of daily life, work, pleasures, housing, the common opinion of friends, the outpourings of the cinema, the press and the wireless. Sooner or later the problem of reconciling life and spirituality arises. And the crisis is especially marked when a young Christian marries and establishes a home. From that moment he should be able to settle himself in a community which is Christian, and is therefore capable of absorbing his whole life and of filling it with the light of grace and faith in Christ. Because this is so difficult we have in many cases to admit failure.

We are drawn, inevitably, to the heart of the problem, which is the rechristianizing of the life of our people at its source. Even though Catholic Action is a privileged instrument of this task, we have to admit that only the parish, the local and the universal seat of the Redemption, can become the adequate means. It is this conviction which has been directing all the pastoral labours of Father Michonneau.

Now when dealing with parishes devoted to this work of rechristianizing, we ought to exploit all that the past can teach us about apostolic conquest, so as not to miss any possible method. Our first task must be to form again an atmosphere of religious life which can spread the message of Christ through every level of life within a particular parish. Only in this way will the masses be won back.

We congratulate Father Michonneau on this important contribution to a new advance of the apostolate in France. He gives a plan, and he also shows results. Hard work and experience have preceded this book, which is the account of the experiences of the priestly team at Colombes and of their contacts with real life. This makes the text concrete in its thoughts, and its realism gives even more weight to its message, which tells of the tremendous religious longings of souls who are waiting only to find a living manifestation of the profound holiness of the Church, before they turn to her.

This account of such a missionary apostolate and of such a pastoral life—totally consecrated to these fundamental problems of our age—cannot fail to make its appeal to the hearts of many priests who are anxious for the spiritual progress of their own parish. And it will awaken many questions in the souls of those who are trying to mould and train themselves for the ministry, and they will come to see the rôle of a diocesan priest in a new light.

A few words may be necessary for those who may believe that they find in this book of Father Michonneau things he never intended to say. It should be evident that shortsighted criticisms are no help to anyone; true charity is always constructive. It is true that the Church down through these long centuries has explained the Redemption and the graces of the Spirit according to the needs of each age, always with the intention of perfecting each age. Our generation should remember that, if it now has before it such a wealth of faith and religion, such a chance to spread the Christian spirit, it owes this to its predecessors. They are the ones who toiled at the work of cultivation and seeding on fields which some precipitate moderns want to plough under.

A real apostle is no mere critic. He is a servant in the work of Christ, and he knows that he is only one link in a long chain of generations; he is eager enough and humble enough to accept the fruits of time-proven wisdom. It may be that certain customs and plans must gradually disappear, to be replaced by others more suitable to our own times, but, at the same time, we must recognize that there was a day when these were useful. We must avoid the childish error that our generation is destined to settle every problem, to reconstruct everything. Even our efforts and methods, good for to-day, may show their inadequacies tomorrow. Let those preparing to become apostles of Christ remember these fundamental truths and refrain from criticism that is as ill-advised as they are inexperienced.

It sometimes happens that we get excited questions about whether or not Father Michonneau's picture of a missionary apostolate does not demand a revision of priestly spirituality, even to the extent of modifying the traditional form of priestly prayer—the Breviary. That was never the aim of this book. Rather, it proposes to revivify these basic practices of prayer-life by means of a constant solicitude for the work of Christ and for the sanctification of the parish. It would truly be shortsighted for anyone to think that he finds any incompatibility between the missionary ideal of a priest who keeps in contact with reality and the demands of the interior life—without which the priest will soon find himself stripped of the spirituality he thought he had. The interior life has its inexorable demands; it must be sustained by intimate converse between the soul and God; it must take part in the common prayer-life of the Church, and the natural expression for this is the Breviary. There are many who, in their sincere desire to radiate the influence of Christ, find these ancient safeguards of the spiritual life burdensome. Such men are merely avoiding the problem, not solving it, when they think that they can accomplish an apostolic task without these same basic elements of apostolic spirituality, mental prayer and the Divine Office.

The demands of this apostolate are not such as to force us to abandon all care for 'culture', as some might think from reading the chapter in this book which is devoted to that problem. What is demanded is that the priest must know how to be approachable, and so he must somehow share in the 'culture' of his people. It may be that Father Michonneau does not make his distinctions clear enough between that illusory familiarity with the popular mind which would result if a priest were to jettison the humane culture which is part of the equipment of a minister of God, and the true adaptation by which a priest can be understanding and be understood without thereby ceasing to elevate and spiritualize the souls entrusted to his care. The first attitude would be a deplorable debasement, and would seriously compromise the efforts of any priest. Only the second is worthy of an apostle bringing Christ back into our world.

xiv

There is no point in deceiving ourselves; the adaptation demands constant effort from all of us. We still have to acquire and use our heritage of sacred sciences, but we must avoid the error of keeping it in the abstract and academic. We must make use of secular sciences too, so as to gain an entrance into the interests of our world and make Christ known in it. In any case, we may be sure that, if people are offended by seeing priests who find it hard to come down to their level, they will be even more hurt to find in us the same common and vulgar limitations they see in themselves.

And finally, it should be clear that apostolic endeavour cannot succeed without constant obedience to the hierarchy which has the task of organizing the whole Christian life of a given area. There are priests who think that daring experiments begun in their own parishes are of concern to no one else but themselves. Now, besides the fact that these rash undertakings seldom produce any lasting good, these priests make the mistake of thinking that obedience to the hierarchy will stifle all boldness in the cause of Christ, all generosity in his service. The reverse is true, and every isolated effort can gain real benefit from the control and support which the heads of the hierarchy, because of their greater vision, can furnish—if there is submission to the over-all work of Christ. As individuals we may come upon a particular solution of particular problems, but we should ask ourselves if we have sufficient vision, if our zeal is in step with the whole Christian community, which the Holy Ghost is guiding. These questions find their answers in constant reference to the judgment of the hierarchy and in constant submission to its decisions.

This does not mean that we should always wait for impetus from above; only laziness would come to that conclusion. But we certainly are obliged to submit our projects to the approval of superiors and to ask for the advice and judgment which obedience to the Church demands. There could not be, for example, any question of altering for some professedly apostolic reason, but without the consent of the hierarchy, customs generally observed in the Church. Some have asked whether or not the wearing of ecclesiastical dress may not be a liability rather than an asset to the apostolate.

One thing to remember in questions like these is that we are poor judges in our own cases; that is why we must submit to truly hierarchical authority.

It should also be evident that no apostolic effort can attain its goal unless the priestly dignity and office are upheld. A priest must grow in the esteem of his people and in the sight of God.

We cite these instances by way of example, and without any intention of making reservations in our opinion of this text, because we are delighted with the book. Our intention is merely to put things in their proper light for all those who wish to take this priestly group at Colombes as a model. May the book of Father Michonneau give rise to new developments in the marvellous Christian activity among working people, and may it shed new light on the zeal of all those who, in every corner of France, are engaged in this work.

August 1, 1946.

✠ EMMANUEL CARDINAL SUHARD,

Archbishop of Paris.

FORETHOUGHTS

I

Abbé Michonneau

A suburban priest makes a poor author.

How will he find time to write? From the time of his Mass, until the end of the last meeting at night, his day is well filled with the care of his flock, visits to be made, tales to hear, business to do.

When, poor man, will he be able to undertake any writing? He has hardly found time to think of it, when his door-bell rings, calling him to solve some immediate problem.

Besides all this, his viewpoint is necessarily limited. Completely given over to this corner of the vineyard which the bishop has entrusted to him, how can he have the broad outlook or do the research that is necessary for writing a book?

And yet, if a parish priest will not speak about parishes and parish ministry, who will?

How often are we parish clergy exasperated on reading the work of some pastoral theologian, because we know that he is expressing only theoretical views. He did not live the life before writing about it. And it is so easy to make up an armchair approach to the ministry!

That is why, after much hesitation, I acceded to the request of Father Maydieu, and put down in black and white my ideas about a parish of working people. That was in 'Rencontres'.[1] But I did refuse to take on the editing of this work, and asked for a collaborator; and so Father Chéry has added his style, as flowing as a Dominican habit, to these thoughts.

I say now that these thoughts are 'our' thoughts, for my curates and I are one. We lived this book together before we came to write it with Father Chéry. It is the result of our common experience and of our lengthy discussions together as a team in contact with reality. That is why,

[1] *Rencontres* is the title of a series of essays and studies which began during the war when *La Vie Intellectuelle*, like all the other periodicals, was forbidden by the Germans. This book is included in the series.

even when it is only the parish priest speaking, it is always 'we', the plural of reality, not of majesty.

Let none of my fellow-priests see in this work the slightest intention of teaching them a lesson. If certain statements sound categoric and others seem sweeping, I ask them to forgive my awkwardness. A man of action is always a little precipitate; he believes in his 'pet theory', gives himself to it, heart and soul, and does not worry much about the finer shades.

It was not my intention in writing these pages to compose a treatise of pastoral theology, and still less to describe a model missionary parish. I was asked about what we had done at Colombes, taking into consideration the circumstances of time, place and persons as they are here; and this is the answer. We might have done differently in the years ahead; as I get old and have other collaborators around me, it is very likely that our methods will evolve, because, as the proverb goes, 'only fools or dead men cannot change'.

So let no one try to find in these pages anything that smacks of hard and fast rules. Parishes are very different one from another. The men whom Christ has chosen to evangelize them are too distinct in nature and grace, and pastoral gifts are psychological factors too diversified for anyone to presume to lay down the last word about methods.

I marvel at those who make up plans for the conversion of parishes or for the penetration of certain classes of society. The only eventuality that they do not foresee is that their plans may never work out.

There will always be a definite rôle for intuition to play in making plans, and even more important and more indispensable is grace. These 'undeterminates' always prevent us from calculating ahead the precise value that any particular parish work will have.

And yet priests from every section of France who have come to see us or who have been asked random questions about our thoughts, have showed that they reached pretty much the same conclusions on many points. They were facing the same problems in about the same perspective as we, and seeing, as did we, the failure of the same timeworn methods, they arrived at similar solutions.

Thus it may be that our pages will have only a general interest, for we do not believe that they are saying anything very new. We only want to bring together ideas that are now scattered and unable to express themselves.

Some, more prudent than we, would no doubt have hesitated before putting forth certain ideas which may seem a little radical, but if anyone needs a shoulder on which to shift the responsibility for such ideas, we will gladly lend him ours.

And, in exchange, we ask our confrères to be good enough to say a prayer that the parish of Sacré Coeur de Colombes may not suffer too much from having a parish priest who deserted them for a while, so as to work on this book.

G. MICHONNEAU
Parish Priest of Sacré Coeur de Colombes.

II

Father Chéry, O.P.

Now a word about the editor of these pages.

When Father Maydieu asked me to work with Father Michonneau, I had no idea of the opportunities being offered me. I came to Colombes on a fine May morning in 1944; pastor and curates were together at a simple meal. In a few minutes I was plunged into a warmly apostolic atmosphere of mission problems, of priestly brotherhood and of supernatural life. Christ was here; Saint Paul was here.

The 'ideas' of Father Michonneau and his co-workers are not mere ideas; I mean they are not living by an ideology. Rather, it is actual parish experience that they have thought out and expressed. In fact, they have a dread of theory. But they are thinking while they live, and it is with joy that they see priests and lay people all over France thinking with them. They have begun to realize the 'mission parish' as they see it. It is not a finished product yet—and never will be. Nothing is more opposed to the very idea of completion than their missionary undertaking. A permanent evolution, a constant adaptation based on actual needs—that is the essence of Sacré Coeur of Colombes.

It is easy to see how this attitude makes for a difficult job. A plan was set up for each chapter. I took notes from a dictation that was more like a conversation. Then I would go off and make a rough draft of what had been said. At the next meeting I would read over this copy, and watch for frowns or approving nods; that would show me where I had become lost in theories: so we revised and revised. Finally, after some months, the book appeared.

This is not a complete work. It is for the reader to follow up what is said here. Let no one judge this book as though it were a text-book of a professor. We are in the midst of life. And it is for this very reason that these proposals of Father Michonneau will reach a large and interested audience. If they provoke readers to write to us, if they occasion contacts or suggestions, they will have fulfilled their purpose. It might even happen that the 'Rencontres' collection will have to put out a new volume to bring these results to our readers.

The outline of this book is simple enough.

We are confronted, as was Abbé Godin,[1] by a pagan proletariat, by that section of France which is truly a 'mission land'. In this land parishes already exist. Providentially they are the mission centres; if they do not accomplish their end, they are failing in their vocation. And they cannot accomplish it by remaining stagnated in an atmosphere of 'faithful parishioners'. They must become *Mission Communities*. That is the theme of the first chapter.

How will they become Mission Communities? Answering that question is the function of the whole book.

By a living and popular liturgy, says Chapter Two.

By the apostolate, says Chapter Three, wherein we take up the study, from a mission point of view, of the value of what are generally called 'parish activities'. We consider different types of specialized movements. Finally, we decide

---

[1] Abbé Godin was one of the founders of the famous *Missions de Paris* which have been winning back the pagans and the communists to the service of Christ in the suburbs of Paris. He has also contributed to a volume in the series *Rencontres* entitled : *France Pays de Mission?*

on the superiority of the 'direct apostolate' by clergy and laity.

Then comes Chapter Four, with a discussion of the pastoral needs which compel us to aim at creating a stir with our parish communities in this dechristianized world of ours, so as to make it face the religious question quite frankly.

A great obstacle stands in the way of priests who are trying to reach the mass of people. It is the 'clink of money around the altar'. Chapter Five tries to form the type of conscience which will end this noise, which drowns the voice of Christ.

Another obstacle, and one to which we generally pay little attention is that of our 'culture'. The object of Chapter Six is to get over the hurdle, especially in preaching.

What is required of apostles to the people is the theme of Chapter Seven; namely an adjusted priestly spirituality, and a spirit of teamwork to bind the priests together and to be extended throughout the parish.

Finally, the last chapter deals with results of the whole plan as worked out at Colombes, and shows that the parish must be ready to receive 'neophytes' which other apostles (e.g. the *Mission de Paris*) direct towards it.

We have written this book in dialogue form in order to keep the direct style of the talks which are the origin of the book, but it will be clear that the questions and answers are the fruit of careful editing.

H. Ch. Chéry, O.P.

I THE PARISH AND THE MISSIONS

Plea for the parish.

In 'An Open Letter to Abbé Daniel', I read, 'You seem to group indiscriminately, under the name of "pagan masses", the totality of those who do not come to church. Allow me to disagree. It is certainly clear, at least in France, that almost all these people are really Christians, that is, they are baptized persons who used to go to church, who have learnt their catechism, who know some priests and who may even have taken part in some parish activities. I will grant that such are mediocre Christians, almost apostates; but, bad as they are, they are not "pagans".'

Do you agree with this view of one of your confrères, a priest in Paris? Is it true that the majority of people is really Christian?

What we think is that all of this is mere playing with words, as regards the title of Christian. If you consider as 'real Christians' everyone who has been baptized, or even only those who made their First Communion and had, in childhood, some degree of contact with the Church, then the problem is solved. The 'mass' in France is Christian; there is no 'mission territory' in France. But if we wish to restrict the title of Christian (and we are not saying 'good Christians') to those who have the Faith, to those to whom Christ is a reality, we must have the courage to stand by the opinion of 'France, a Mission Land', and that the mass of the working class *is* pagan. Not because they do not practise the Faith, but because (and the evidence is so clear on this point that we are amazed at any discussion of it), their mentality is pagan and completely foreign to the Christian spirit, indifferent to our creed and careless of the demands of our moral code. Let a child of this group make his First Communion, let him be married at church, let him call on a priest to bury his dead (and many do not even do that), and yet, all of that does not really change him much. Behind all these appearances, behind this exterior ritualism, the heart of these people is pagan. And so we must approach them in a different way. The method must be different; it must be missionary, for this portion of our country is a mission territory.

1

Will this class become apostates?

We no longer think so. An apostate, essentially, is one who denies a doctrine he once held to adhere to a new one. He leaves a Church of which he once was a member, and he is aware of this abandonment. There is nothing like that in the lives of our modern infidels. Our youngsters who never go back to any practice of religion after their First Communion day are not conscious of any true apostasy. Their parents, who have ceased practising their religion, which they used to practise in Brittany or the Vendeé, are perhaps aware of a certain negligence. When we realize the irreligious atmosphere in which children are steeped from their earliest years and the force of the stream that is carrying each one of them along, we also realize that it is impossible to determine guilt in the fault that they commit. Furthermore, we have to see that the mentality of their surroundings completely conquers them, after a few years of factory work, or even of office work. The anti-religious, or rather, pagan attitude, is so strong in the factories and offices that the mentality of those who have been baptized, and whom some would like to call 'real Christians', is no different from that of the non-baptized. The conduct of both is the same. We can consider both as pagans.

Yet there is something in the affirmation of our confrère of which we must not lose sight, not so much in his use of the term, but in the consequences which flow from it, and in the conclusions we can reach about it. Often we have dealings with people who used to practise their religion, and who used to have some contact with us. Despite what we said above, there is more than a spark of Faith left in them, and this gives us some hope that they may be influenced by the parish.

How is that?

First of all, since the great majority of our people come into contact with us at some time or other, there must be a way of using this contact. And since the parish is the intermediary by which they get into touch with priests, it follows that the parish must play a part in evangelizing them.

So, let us have the courage to admit that:

1. Since, as things are now, the only evident result of

their relations with us is that it keeps their indifference alive, it follows that our methods have to be checked if not completely changed.

2. Here and now the fact of having had some contact with priests is something that people cannot erase from their lives—memories, impressions, direction of ideas, and even certain habits kept through life—all these make up a web on which the parish can work. A slender web, often invisible—Abbé Godin saw that —but it is something still there, and it is the basis of our hopes for the parish apostolate.

Here, then, our first conclusion: we have to deal with a parish which is a mission parish in a mission land.

Is that so in the section you have to evangelize?

If we tell you that it is situated on the outskirts of the Department of the Seine and that almost all its inhabitants are workers, that should answer you. That should tell you that almost everyone here is a pagan.

In this population there are individuals who keep up the religious practices they learned in the provinces; but these are the older women, a few men, and any children whom we may have gathered into some parish society. So it is new parish territory for us, though not as unworked as are many sections of our Parisian suburbs.

Here are a few figures. There are about 22 or 23 thousand inhabitants, and, five years ago, we used to see one thousand at Sunday Mass. Every year since, we have seen an increase of approximately 10 per cent.; so, in 1945, when the evacuees come back, we can expect to have from 1400 to 1500 persons in the church for all the Sunday Masses. During our district missions, in one district, we found only 40 families out of 800-1000, in which we priests knew even one member as practising. In another district, out of the same number of families that we visited, 117 were represented at the mission on the first night; and of these 117, 82 families were completely unknown to us and had not even one practising member. All of this means that the percentage of practising Catholics among us is about 5 per cent. You can see that we agree with Abbé Godin, whom some consider too pessimistic.

3

The only reason we hesitate to give examples of the pagan spirit is that their frequency and number make them commonplace. Any parish priest has a stock of them; any of our visitors can cite some to you, because, being visitors and less hardened than we, they notice the paganism more. An example of this was given by the small boy who came to the priest for First Communion classes. When the priest asked for his father's name, so as to put it down in the register, the youngster innocently replied: 'None, right now, but we're looking around for one'. The same outlook is shown by many mothers who, when speaking about their children to us, never mention the child's character or disposition, but always find the height of praise in such remarks as: 'How sweet he is', or 'How cute', or 'What sturdy legs he has'. It was such a mother as this whom we were trying to console when she lost her child; we did our best to speak about the happiness of the innocent soul in heaven, but the mother kept moaning out her grief in terms like these: 'He was so chubby' and 'What a beautiful child he was'.

When people come to make arrangements about Baptism, First Communion or Marriage, they often make remarks that show up their point of view, as if these meant nothing. 'Oh, if you only didn't have to have Baptisms before breakfast!' 'You know how it is. If his catechism marks are going to look bad on his report-card, I'd just as soon not have him make his First Communion'. 'If you won't marry my boy-friend and me without making us wait for eight days, then we won't be married in Church'. 'I want to be married by a priest, but if it has to be in the sacristy, it's simply not worth the trouble'.

Throughout this book we shall have occasion to cite other examples which will show the condition of the religious and moral values of our poor people. But let us repeat now, so as to make ourselves clear: there is no difference between real pagans (those who have had no contact with religion), and those semi-apostates who have been re-paganized, and who are totally different from true Christians.

Do you think that these pagans can be drawn by Christianity?

The answer to this question is a difficult one. There is little religious sentiment in these people, and so there is a

4

lack of adequate response to real Christianity. And yet they are not totally indifferent to religious problems, because things like the existence of a hereafter, the explanation of suffering, the person of Christ, etc., catch their attention and interest, once such things are presented to them.

Does that mean that they can easily be attracted towards the Church?

Not at all. They will willingly let themselves be drawn by the mystical side of Christianity, but they are decidedly rebellious when it is a matter of practices. The positive law of the Church leaves them indifferent, even hostile. If you will forgive the use of a barbarism, we are of the opinion that they are easily 'Christifiable' but not yet 'Ecclesiasticable'.

Two factors make the christianization of the masses more difficult than conversions in the early ages or in savage lands. Bringing the Gospel to ancient Rome was possible partly because it was merely a question of a change. The pagans had a religion; the State had a religion; the gods were a topic of everyday conversation; and there was public, official worship. In our days religion has vanished from the hearts of our people; they consider it as something outworn, dead. When we try to bring them back to a practice of it, it is as though we were recalling a thing of the past. Hence the task is more difficult now than it was in the time of the Apostles. Besides, the pagans of Rome or the savages to which our foreign missioners go, are people accustomed to obedience; they recognize authority and are submissive to superiors. Not so our modern Western pagan; he is a fierce advocate of equality. He does not want to obey. So, when it comes to embracing a religion and accepting two authorities—God who makes laws, and the Church which teaches in his name—there is difficulty. All of our militant Christians, and especially those of the 'Mission de Paris' have spoken to us of the difficulty (which we too have experienced) of forming a spirit of obedience to authority.

How often, in the missions we were holding at the church, we felt complete agreement between our audience and ourselves whilst we were talking about Christ, his social

5

doctrine, or the moral worth of the Gospel. And yet it was always impossible, for the time being, to expect more than that. How often we have heard women, and even men, tell us that they pray at home or at work sometimes. With complete sincerity, they tell us that they are believers, that they would not dream of missing Mass on All Saints' Day or Palm Sunday; that they absolutely never eat meat on Good Friday, and so God must be pleased with them. Poor training? It certainly is. But the thing to notice is the distance between their mentality and ours; the lack of a sense of obedience enabling them to accept obligation; the resistance to 'clerical domination'; and, above all, the lack of an understanding of our rites, our dogmas, our demands. There is no evident effect from our liturgy, preaching or influence. And remember that we are speaking here of semi-Christians, and not of the pagan majority.

Let us learn how to be patient, and how to approach this task in the right way. We always set up the standards of the Fifth Lateran Council, which determined that the norm of piety for Christians must be at least attendance at Sunday Mass and the reception of the Eucharist at Eastertide. But we must realize that that norm has not yet been attained. That standard was made for Christians who knew what Mass and Communion meant, who recognized the authority of the Church and the necessity of submitting to her laws. Our people are more like those of apostolic times, when the pressing need was to show them Christ, to draw them to spontaneous gatherings, to convince and stir them, before organizing and directing them.

Our task, then, is to create an atmosphere, and this is principally a task for the parish as a whole. The parish should be full of mutual kindness and charity, devout and proud of the Christian name.

Not that that is all, because we do not mean that we have given up hope of one day attracting converts to the practice of religion. We do insist, however, that it is foolish to hope to attract them without a long preparation, without a change in their present mentality. It is false to measure their willingness to accept Christ by their unwillingness to come to Mass. Many priests make that very mistake, and consequently we must take special pains to avoid it; it is nothing but 'putting the cart before the horse' to invite to Mass people who have no Christian values. To judge the progress or failure of our efforts at evangelization by the number of people who appear at Mass is a very poor method of judging. That attendance is not only secondary (*in ordine intentionis*), but also second (*in ordine exsecutionis*). We cannot 'shanghai' these people; their participation must come from a true need of religion. Hence, our apostolate must aim, not at organizing those who already are practising Catholics and who go to Mass and the Sacraments, but rather, to penetrate the different milieus with the spirit of Christianity, so that the need for a Christian life will drive them to Christ, who is communicated to us by the Church and the Sacraments.

Our contention that these souls are 'Christifiable', but not 'Ecclesiasticable', should not cause any apostle to become discouraged; it merely points out the proper approach.

Do you consider this transition from a pagan spirit to a Christian one an individual or a collective phenomenon?

A collective one, certainly. And for the reason that, as Abbé Godin pointed out, and as we shall have occasion to observe later, the majority of our people think only collectively. Only a small percentage is capable of individual thought, and it is these who discuss and reflect on social and religious questions. The others, the great majority, are not aware of any personal capabilities along such lines; they are submerged in the vague 'personality' of the group to which they belong. They think as a unit and subscribe only to those ideas which the group holds, whether that group is their Union, their fellow-workers, their political party or their friends. Hence it is impossible to draw them to Christ as individuals. Either the whole group goes over to him, or no one does. The conquest must be a collective one. That does not mean a conquest of the entire working class (which 'class' is an entity, but not a reality), but of *this* group, of *this* portion here and now.

We must bend and direct the mentality of this particular group or district. If the clergy become well thought of, if parish life and activity are brought into the light, if everyone hears about the different feasts and ceremonies, if families really live like Christians, if militant Christians bring to different services people who had not even realized that such things went on, if, in short, we use a team spirit and a network of Christian action, then we are creating an atmosphere, and the parish is already playing an important rôle. Maybe the pastor will not see any increase at the processions held on the first Sunday of every month, but his people are nearer to Christ.

What conclusions do you draw from all this?

It means that our efforts will proceed along two approaches. For the small class of 'thinkers', we will work on their compact family circles. For the others, the vast majority, we must go out and win over the entire group among whom they work and live.

Who is to make these efforts?

Both the parish with its priests and active laity, and the 'Mission de Paris', or its equivalent. We shall come back to the part the latter has to play.

So you think that the parish has a place in this conquest?

Absolutely! *A parish in a mission country must be a missionary parish.* It cannot confine itself to the spiritual needs of the Christian people. Naturally part of its activity will be meant especially for them—but only a part, and that not the most important. Since 95 per cent. of our people do not come to us, we must direct 95 per cent. of our efforts to them. Not merely by sighs and vain wishes, but by real activity.

What do you mean when you say 'the parish'?

This is an important point. A parish may be considered as a conservative, or as a conquering force. According to whether we adopt one or the other meaning shall we be able to make our parish 'missionary'; otherwise, we might as well give up the idea. This distinction seems to us to be essential to what will be said in this book, so we shall be insistent on it.

The first meaning: for some (and inasmuch as most of us do not react against routine, we usually fall into this category) the parish means the sum total of all those who come to church. 'My parishioners', a priest will say. In this sum total we can distinguish several groups: first of all, the few really faithful ones who receive Communion every day or every Sunday, and who are the backbone of all parish activity; then, those who come to Mass every Sunday, and whom the priest knows at least slightly; next, the type which comes to church for the big feasts, if only to offer their pious mite of worship, because, as they will tell you, 'they are on the Church's side'; lastly, the border-line group of those who are well-disposed, in a sense, to religion, who have their children baptized and instructed for First Communion, who come to the church to be married (usually), who call for a priest at their deathbeds, and who hold to church burial as to a family custom.

So according to this conception the parish means all those who have some contact with the Church, with whom the priest has some connection—even if these relations show a great similarity to commercial ones of some special nature.

Parish life becomes the cultural life of souls such as these. Its basis is the calendar of feast-days and Sundays. Its manifestation is found in ceremonies, baptisms, marriages, processions, funerals, various meetings at the church or parish hall, triduums, retreats, and Lenten services.

The mainstays of such a parish are its societies which supply the various reservoirs on which we can depend when it is necessary to organize things for some big feast, or where we can go for help in forming special groups—such as youth activities, sodalities, men's groups, or ladies' clubs.

The clergy, pastor and curates, must divide their time between ministering to these souls according to their spiritual needs and taking care of temporal affairs. And this latter becomes more and more burdensome according to the number of the activities, and according to the prosperity and growth of the parish.

Hence this concept means that parish and the parish milieu are identical.

In the rural areas, a parish is usually considered as being just what you have described. But in a city or suburban parish, making contact with immense numbers of pagans, 'parish' surely must have another meaning.

Unfortunately, it does not. The illusion is ever easier and even more widespread in our suburban and city parishes

9

than it is in less densely populated or rural areas. In the country a priest wittingly has to think of those who do not come to church, and to enter into contact with them. First of all, his small flock does not take up all his time; and with regard to the others, he meets them every day in the streets. He knows them and they know him. While the number of practising Catholics in city parishes is not more than a tiny fraction of all those who live within the parish, it still is a number sufficiently large to occupy all our time; and—which is worse—it prevents us from seeing the others who do not come near us.

In our suburban parishes, even more than in the rural areas, you will find the very essence of this parish spirit spoken of above. Parish life here, more than in any other place, is reduced to the ordinary life of the people. The smaller the proportion of faithful to the number of the indifferent, the more is this noticeable. In the country those who come to church usually represent good people of all classes. Here, since the pagan proletariat is a tremendous majority, the contrast between parish life is reduced to conform to the milieu, and the life which goes on in this particular district is more marked. A full church at Sunday Mass should not lull us into thinking that all is well; let us look at realities.

It is easy enough for the clergy to be kept busy with the faithful flock. The church will look full enough, and services and activities will be well attended. The priests will think that they are reaching the masses because of this large number, and they will think that they have here the real reactions of the people; in reality they are reaching only the 'parish milieu'. They will think that they are succeeding because their ministry is bringing them satisfaction. In reality, they have no contact at all with the masses.

Another factor clouds our perspective. We tend to judge the parish by the contacts we have in the church or sacristy, with those who come about their children, or to arrange a marriage. We are wrong. Those who come to see us—especially if they are ordinary folk—come with an attitude of inferiority, even servility. They talk like us; but they do not think like us. And the real hardened cases never come

10

to see us. How often, in our visits around the parish, we have been conscious of that complex of servility in families who had a child in our catechism class. We could see it in their very welcome. We realized that we were to give the decision whether or not their child should be admitted to his First Communion; they were flattering us. They would not dream of contradicting us in whatever we might say.

Besides all this, another enormous difficulty in parishes like ours is knowing our parishioners and remembering their names—let alone trying to look for them in church. And hence it is an easy step to begin to misconstrue their attitude, to make no effort to understand their mentality, and even to forget about those whom we no longer see around the church. Evangelization here is a terrible problem. It hurts us to think about those whom we must reach; forgetting about them is easier.

What about the other meaning of a 'parish'?

The other concept consists in this. Having studied a map of the parish, or—better still—after having made a walking tour of the whole place, we say to ourselves: Our parish is this entire territory; all those living inside this section are committed to our care, without any exception made because of nationality or immorality or hostility to the clergy. Nothing can free us from the obligation of caring for their souls. Hence all those who do not come to us, and whom we will never get to know unless we go to them; all those we meet—including Algerians and Chinese—they are all our parishioners. We have to say to ourselves, 'We, their priests, have the care of these souls'.

Our parish life should inform the life of all these people; the spiritual life of those who have any (and how can we tell if a spark is not still there, even in those who seem most distant?); their workaday life; their life at home, at rest. That life is made up of the very air that they breathe, the things that occupy them, the joys and sorrows they have known, the influences which play upon them—the influence of the doctor who tends them, of the paper that interprets the world for them, of the leaders who direct them, of the public house at the street corner, of the theatre which sees them more often than the church does.

Our parish . . . we see it at noon, when the factory lets
out its workers; at mid-afternoon, when the children get
out of school; in the morning, when buyers line up outside
the shops; in the evening when the suburban trains roll in
with wave after wave of our people; at night, with the
young fellows and girls on the corners.

This is our parish, and we must recognize that fact, for
souls are at stake.

Does not every priest feel the same way?

In theory they do. In practice how many act according
to the logic which such a theory demands?

We have not reached the point of reversing the numbers
given by our Lord in the famous parable; that is, we do not
say that ninety-nine sheep have left the fold, and one faithful
one remains. And yet we remember a saying of one of our
professors in the seminary: 'We do not go after the lost
sheep any more. We let them run off to the hills, these
ninety-nine lost ones, while we argue about who is going to
be allowed to fondle the one that is left.'

This comes about because we confuse in practice the
Kingdom of God with our own kingdom—the advance of
God's reign with our own influence over a flock. What does
it matter if it is small, as long as we have it well in hand?

*Still, is it not Utopian to be forever thinking about those who do
not come near us, and forgetting those upon whom we can count?
Is not the old proverb true which tells us first to conserve what we
have, before we try to conquer anything new?*

No! Open the Gospel. Whether we want it so or not,
however hard or impractical it might appear, we are only
obeying Christ when we busy ourselves more about those
afar off; and, if we let ourselves forget these separated ones
while we tend the faithful little flock, there is nothing
evangelical about us. Maybe the Gospel is not practical;
maybe it is a little idealistic sometimes. I remember a
parish priest saying to me one day: 'My dear friend, we can
hardly expect to apply the Gospel nowadays'. And yet
was it not by purely evangelical methods that Saint Paul
and the other apostles transformed the world? Might it not
be by our too reasonable methods that we are running the
risk of letting this world perish? Anyhow, it is not so certain

that we do have to abandon the faithful in order to run after the lost sheep. It may well be a matter of getting our faithful to be with us and like us in the pursuit of the others. We shall come back to this point too.

What is certain, and what we really want to emphasize, is that the way we think of a parish is of paramount importance in deciding its part in the missionary movement.

If the parish is no more than a central rallying point for Christians, a place where the faithful gather for services and meetings and activities, then, whether this attitude is based on theory or a mere acceptance of things as they are, we have to admit that the parish is not capable of attracting the 98 per cent. of the working class which does not know Christ. We will have to leave it to specialized missionaries to take up work among them.

But if, on the contrary, we strip off routine and turn boldly to new forms of the apostolate, the parish becomes a living cell, destined to propagate itself over an entire district. Then we can see that it has its rôle to play in this missionary endeavour.

Do you think that the parish can play this part?

Without a doubt. Firstly, because it is already existing. Whether it plays its rôle or not, *hic et nunc*, the parish is a fact. It is, by right, if not in reality, that tiny cell of Christianity, of the Incarnation, about which we are talking. Whatever be its future, the parish is, right now, the one concrete element of the task of evangelization.

If we look at a whole territory like France, or even just Paris and the suburbs, we have to admit that the network of parishes is admirably suited to the task ahead of us. Every community has its own. Not even the civil government is as well organized, for many a district has several parishes. One of our pet ideas is that there are not enough parishes, that we must multiply them; and the building of new churches has shown clearly that parish organization is not only a fine framework, but also a supple one, which can be enlarged indefinitely.

So it is something that the parish *is* and that there is no question about its existence, or right to existence. It is no small thing to know that something is, when others have to figure out what is going to be. It is no small gain that the parish is recognized, solidly rooted, instead of being a novelty which could be attacked.

And that is not all, for a parish is equipped. It has its priests, and parish clergy have always been the mainstay of the Church's force. They are the ones who always have borne the brunt of the burden, wherever the bishop might send them; they represent the Church in the eyes of the people. They live in the midst of those whom they are evangelizing. They are, or can be, or should be, in permanent contact with their people. They are the ones whom everyone sees in the streets, whom everyone greets, knowing very well that they alone have the authority to carry out the chief functions of common Christian life.

And if, besides considering the number of these priests, we realize the actual set-up in each parish, we shall see what power and influence these parish priests and curates— all occupied by the same sort of problem, and all striving in different places for the one great goal of the apostolate— could wield. Unfortunately, we say 'could' and not 'do'.

A scene from the J.O.C. Congress of 1937 comes to mind here. Seeing the crowds of youths surrounding their chaplains, the secretary of the Socialist Youth Club leaned towards Abbé Godin and said: 'You certainly have the chaplains. If we had as many men who would dedicate themselves to making militants of the rest of us, you would see us get somewhere.'

And parish priests are even more numerous than are these J.O.C. chaplains. Add to them the number of nuns who work in parishes (more than 5000 in the Archdiocese of Paris!); add to this the number of lay persons who are entirely occupied with different parish activities. Then the question is not 'What can the parish do?' but, 'Why hasn't it done more?'

And this is not all. Every parish has militants in all sorts of movements—marvellous Christians, whose influence is enormous. And it has all the faithful, who live in the midst of the ordinary people and whose lives could be and should be lived round the parish life.

Materially speaking, every parish has its church, and

14

that is no small advantage. Here is a reality which even the most uninterested can hardly ignore. It may well be that many a person has never set foot inside the church, but it is more probable that most have, at one time or another. In any case, it is there, for all to see, as a witness and symbol of something which they are ignoring, or, worse still, misunderstanding. For all, even confusedly, it means something.

A parish has some sort of a hall or meeting-place, too, and God knows how much energy has been expended these last fifty years to build them up. Maybe they are never filled; maybe they are, in the minds of many, places to stay away from. At least they are a means of gathering some people, and perhaps they could be made to appear different from the rest.

A parish has revenues, no matter how small or how large, how steady or how sporadic.

It has means of expression—magazines, bulletins, announcements—and the pulpit is always available.

Above all, it has official recognition as the instrument of missionary work in a particular sector. It is a continuation of the Christian communities which the Acts of the Apostles tells us were established everywhere that the apostles went; and it is to this community that new converts in the area are joined. Hence if a parish abandons, theoretically or practically, the task of announcing Christ to the mass of men in its territory, it is failing in its mission, it is betraying the mandate it received. Let specialists come in, if they are needed; that is normal enough; but to leave the infidels to these specialists and concern oneself only with the faithful —that is thwarting the will of Christ. And if these special helpers are not being used, the obligation of aiming at these infidels rests even more heavily on the parish.

To sum it all up: the parish is like a mother-cell, the source of all apostolic work. In the future—supposing the task of conquest is over and won—it is to the parish that all the new cells must be joined in a common life. Let us imagine, for a moment, a splendid catechumenate (and we have much to say on this point, too); keep it as distinct as you wish from the body of the faithful, and yet it will still be

15

necessary, once the catechumens are ready, that they should join up with the faithful. Strictly, they probably can find the necessities of spiritual nourishment outside the parish, but for official acts like baptisms, weddings, funerals, where will they come but to the parish?

From this flows the duty and urgent need that the parish be ready to welcome new converts. We shall come back to this.

A parish must be ready to accept any aids which may come to it; there should be a place offered to any person who comes forward to assist in the work, no matter where they come from.

However generous or forceful or ingenious may be specialized methods, it will always be the parish which represents the main strength of the attack, like the infantry of an army. Like the infantry, it will be beaten if it fails to use new armaments and tactics, but it remains the indispensable means of winning and holding any point of attack.

Parish Milieu or Community Milieu?

Do you think that the Parish can play the part you have indicated?
Yes,—but only if it undergoes a bold transformation.
In what sense do you consider this transformation necessary?
The chapters to come will give the details, but for now we would say this. First: everyone must take an active part in the work, because none of the proposed reforms, taken by themselves, can succeed; it is teamwork which will bring victory to the parish. Secondly: the whole point can best be expressed by the formula that 'the parish must cease to be a mere parish milieu; it must become again a community'.

What prevents a parish from being a missionary power? The fact that it is now reduced to the parish environment, which envelops and stifles it; it gives the illusion of vitality, but it is false, or at least, circumscribed, vitality. What will make the parish a missionary force again? Only the fact of its becoming a community again.

What do you mean by all that?
Read the Acts of the Apostles; it describes a crisis in the new-born Church which is amazingly similar to that of our own times.

What do we read there? As the Lord had commanded, the Gospel had been preached to the Jews first; the first of the 'brethren' were from the synagogue, and naturally they kept to their customs, their attachment for the Law of Moses, the distinction of clean and unclean foods, legal purifications, circumcision, etc. They made a synthesis of their normal way of living and their new-found faith in Jesus Christ. But soon the pagans were attracted by the preaching of Christianity and entered into the new communities. Saint Peter baptized the centurion, Cornelius, at Caesarea; the Hellenistic Jews at Cyprus made conquests among the pagans of Antioch. Then Saint Paul arrived to spread the movement, from Antioch into the whole of Asia Minor, Greece, etc. Immediately there arose the difficulty of how and under what conditions to receive these new Gentile converts. The diehards among the Jewish Christians, not being able to dream of any salvation without some connection with the Chosen People, wanted to impose the Mosaic observances on all. A more moderate group was willing to omit this condition, but insisted that they themselves should keep the observances. Even Saint Peter, at Antioch, got up from the table of Gentile converts, to eat with the converts from Judaism, so as not to offend the diehard group. It was Saint Paul who corrected him, and so forcefully proclaimed the 'liberty of the children of God'. If the Law of Moses is going to be foisted on converts from paganism, we might as well abandon preaching the Gospel. Faith in Christ is enough; the Christian way of life is enough. If, furthermore, the distinction about foods is going to be kept up, the destruction of Christian unity will result. Saint Paul won the day, and at the Council of Jerusalem it was decided not to burden the Gentiles with a load they could not carry. As Mgr Batiffol put it, 'the world would never have become Jewish'. For quite a while, the converts from Judaism were to keep their customs, but soon, being a minority, they were absorbed into the majority of pagans who were being converted. Then there arose communities that were simply Christian, in which all elements were fused. The world was to become Christian.

Why did you bring up that crisis?

Because it is the prototype of all the other crises which the Church has ever experienced and especially of the one we are now going through. We, who live in the midst of the common people, can transpose Mgr Batiffol's words into 'the world will never become parochial'—at least not in that sense of 'parish' which we have just been developing. There would be an incompatibility, an incongruity in it. Either the parish would remain enclosed in what we have called the 'parish milieu', while the rest of the world stays outside; or else the parish is to blossom out into a true 'community'. Then there will be another crisis, caused by the difficulties, protests and tugging of dead weight and routine. However, if Saint Paul carries the day again, the people will become Christian.

What do you include in this 'community' you talk about?

Remember those first Christian communities! What were they? Merely groups in which charity and simplicity reigned. Tent-makers dwelt along with doctors; servants with ladies of high society. As Saint Paul put it, there was 'no longer Greek or Jew, slave or free', for, while each lived according to his own station, they were 'all one in Christ Jesus'. Everybody used to say 'Brother', and they really meant it, for they had 'but one heart and one mind'. They used to come together for fraternal meals and the 'breaking of the Bread'. By the sheer strength of their faith and constancy under persecution, but most of all by the love they had for each other, they were real witnesses of Christ whom they professed. They were not recognized by the 'culture' in which they lived, but by the love with which they loved one another, in the love of the same God. Since they were all recent converts, they were dynamic and convert-minded. These Athenian philosophers, these old leaders of the synagogue, these people from the lowlands of Corinth or Ephesus—they all were formed into a completely new sort of unity. As Father Lebreton wrote: 'The Church took to itself all these recruits. Once baptized, they all were but one Body, the Body of Christ, no matter what were their origins. This is what gave the Christian community its deep unity, its essentially religious character. Birth did not give it, nor education, nor the free choice of human

18

attractions; it came through faith, by which the neophyte, being joined to Christ, took unto himself all Christians, his members.'

By this faith and charity they were like a leaven in the old pagan world. An unknown apologist of the third century could say, 'As the soul is to the body, so Christians are to the world'. So effective was this leaven that, in three centuries, these Christian communities had invaded and overthrown all the levels of society in all the Roman Empire.

Are our parishes no longer communities like these?

You have but to observe our parishes for a while, especially one in a pagan environment.

Come into a church on any Sunday morning for the parish High Mass. What do you see? Children, a few nuns, a few women and old men, and a group of choir girls. How many adults between the ages of twenty and fifty? How many men? How many of those who are at the prime of life, and who are really 'alive'? At earlier Masses, who are these pious ladies you see at Communion? What standing do they have in their neighbourhood, in their family, at their work? What enthusiasm do they have? What influence? What natural qualities? How about the late Masses, around noon, and the people we see there? At these, the situation is reversed; there are plenty of men and women who are in the prime of life—but what sort of Christianity do they profess? What interest do they have in the Gospel? What do they represent to the common folk; they are individuals of another class and type, who happen to live amongst the masses of this quarter?

We must not exaggerate. We do know of parishes where young people and entire families are really alive to the natural and supernatural values in life, and they put their Christian vitality into action. But such are extremely few. More often the parish means nothing, and they think of it along lines which we have already mentioned. Other communal groups have given them vitality, but they do not find in the parish that spirit of early Christianity in which they can expand. If (and we do not mean to be unjust, for we realize the spirit of the times) the parish does mean something, and if the efforts of the clergy have been directed

19

to this goal, that same clergy will be the first to lament over what we are lamenting, and the first to rejoice where we rejoice. After all we ourselves are parish priests, and we know that many a priest thinks just as we do. As a matter of fact, this realization led us to publish this book.

Whoever has preached a special sermon for Christian mothers knows the discouragement which comes over us, as we look out at the great number of grandmothers who willingly come to hear us; but we look in vain for the women who might find some profit in the words so carefully prepared for them. And the Christian fathers! Where are they? We see these men, or at least a minority of them, during the three sermons of the Easter retreat, and approximately the same number of them at the back of the church for Mass on Easter Sunday—but when will we see them again? How can we capture them? What are we going to do about them? How many do we never see, retreat or no retreat!

The parish milieu! The Children of Mary, in their veils and blue ribbons, the catechism children, the ladies of the League, a few of the 'good' young people, a few of the men of one sodality or another! In middle-class parishes the fairly large number of fine families which do turn out hides the absence of the great majority which does not come. In the 'working class' parishes there is no such deception; we see the absence.

Faithful followers of Christ are always a minority. These numerical comparisons are no true indication.

Granted! Especially on certain feast days, and we are happy in the numbers. Even if we grant, for now, that it is all right to be happy about this, let us go further, and ask a few questions. What is the worth, as Christians, of this crowd that we see in church? Do they love one another? Are they a unified element of the community? Do they even know one another? Once out of the church, what ideas will they exchange, what influence on one another will they have? Do they have the idea of belonging to one and the same living Body, of being members of one another? Has the ceremony they have just come away from united their minds and hearts in the one, identical hope and thought? Do they go out with the burning desire of making Christ

20

fill their lives and of seeing him reign in their environment? Did they come to fulfil an obligation for their own salvation, or did they come to strengthen and feed a life which they want to spread? What kind of an example are they going to be to the great mass of indifferent souls among whom they live? Will they be a family recognized for its charity, loyalty, faith in Christ, confidence, joy, courage under hardships? Or will they be pretty much like everyone else around them, except for a weekly habit peculiar to them? When others look at this band of the faithful, will they have a mind to become Christian? Is it not more often just the opposite—'If that is being a Christian! No thanks. Not for me!'

Let us go a little farther. Take the hypothesis of a conversion. I do not mean the conversion of some intellectual who has come to accept Christianity; he would be accepted with open arms. What I mean is the conversion of some militant Communist, who had been a zealous anticlerical— or the conversion of some streetwalker who had been a public scandal. How would they be welcomed? Oh, we accept Mary Magdalene, because she is in the Gospel, but I should like to see her walk into one of our meetings! We read about the reluctance with which the Christian Jews of Jerusalem received Saul the persecutor, when he appeared before them as a neophyte,—and we find their attitude astonishing; I should like to see him drop into one of our men's groups! And if this Saul were to multiply himself by ten and invade this parish mentality, causing havoc by his strange attitude—what a disaster! 'Things are not what they used to be in the parish.' Is it not true that the attitude of Catholics to a convert is, almost instinctively, the attitude of the elder brother to the prodigal son, who has finally come home?

It seems to me that you are forgetting the Jocists.

No, we are not. The question is—how have they been welcomed in certain parishes? Were they supported? Are they recognized as a model of what Catholics ought to be : concerned about life, about the atmosphere around them, about their relation to Christ? Or is it not more true to say that they are considered as an unusual type, as people to be tolerated because of their evident goodwill and sincerity, but hardly in step with the parish.

But why do Catholics, taken as a whole, lack this Christian vitality?

Unfortunately it is our fault! We are not overlooking the tremendous influence exerted by the materialism and sensuality which have spread through all our institutions, all our lives; but we are responsible for the weak fight that our faithful make against these influences. Have we not reduced our parishioners to the status of being mere listeners to the sermons, even in organizations where *they* are supposed to do the talking? Are they not obliged to bear with our proposals, advice, commands, without a chance of showing their own ideas? Do we not act more like superiors than guides? We complain about their passivity, but where in the world could they get any ideas of activity? Even those who are very active and successful in their own fields and on a purely natural plane, have become, because of us, people who, when they are around the church, merely receive, preserve, and sometimes defend, the teachings of Christ. They do not give anything; they are passive beings. The parish has become the business of the clergy; it is of no concern to the faithful. They are asked to give money often enough, but never given a say in the use which is made of the money. What is worse, they are kept barred from the apostolate. Yes, we tell them—since Pius XI said so—they have a duty of undertaking Catholic Action, that they must be apostles. But what means do we give them to this end? What initiative do we encourage in them? What part of the work is deliberately and systematically given them? Sometimes youth movements do blossom out, but our timidity in allowing them to do so is something to see. We are a hindrance where we should be a help. Besides all this, think of the many who are not engaged or interested in any of these movements; what are we doing for them?

You are summing up the reflections made by the youth of the Church.

That is correct. Maybe you also read the article 'Has Christianity softened mankind'.

Evidently the answer is 'No' if it is a question of the Christianity of Christ, but, alas! what distinctions will we have to make, if it is a question of the kind of Christianity which we all too often present, who can deny that there is some truth in quotations like the following, taken at random from the above article: 'We might compare the Church to an over-anxious mother, who, lest her children fall into some gully, keeps them at home, in a state of childishness or pseudo-innocence which prevents them from becoming adults'. 'It is all too evident that a certain kind of religious education has produced, especially among the so-called "upper classes", a weak sort of man, scrupulous and even timorous, scared by his own shadow, too thoroughly tied to the apron strings of the Church.' 'It seems that, generally speaking, everything connected with Catholicism has to shake off that heavy, enervating atmosphere which has succeeded in watering down its great truths, weakening their sense, hiding their deep and health-giving reality. Thanks be to God, Catholicism is not always expressed by Sulpician imagery, of which the least we can say is that it shows neither strength nor character, but rather a tendency towards an inoffensive neutrality. We must not let Saint Thérèse become a sweet and timid young thing; we must stop misusing phrases like "a good little child", or "a fine young man". Spiritual directors are not firm enough, and do not know how to get rid of the old ladies and old spinsters who clutter up the sacristies, and cause priests to lose so much precious time.'

Why continue quotes like these? Everyone who thinks a bit and is honest must agree with them. Even though splendid exceptions can be shown (and the ones we know give us hope), it still does not detract from the value of the whole argument. The parish atmosphere is not that of a community; it has none of the dynamism of early Christianity; it has no power to cut into the pagan world in the midst of which it vegetates. Some individuals have left their natural environment and have come into this artificial one—this colourless and lifeless thing we call the 'parish milieu'; they have been given a sort of 'ecclesiastical tinge', which amounts to their becoming bourgeois. But, if they

23

were already bourgeois of a 'high class', they will not feel at ease with this tinge, for they fancy themselves somewhat superior culturally. If they were of the working class, they do not feel at ease either, but realize that they are on foreign ground both here and in their former milieu. What do they find here? The type of person who is engrossed in 'pious works', devout and willing enough, but absolutely useless for the apostolic conquest or for the infiltration into the masses of the pagan proletariat—which is our chief concern.

Well? How can the parish become a community again; how can it become the early Christian type which is necessary for the missionary labour it must do?

That is the problem, and it is tremendous. We do not pretend to have found the solution; we realize its urgency, and we know that thousands of priests and lay people are asking themselves the same questions that we are. In the following chapters, we will attempt a modest presentation of the ideas which came to us; but we repeat, and will continue to repeat: it will be useless for anyone to attempt any of the reforms which we propose, if he goes at them as though they were text-book lessons or exercises. There are plenty of suggestions which can be made; we only hope that this book will stimulate some. May these other suggestions, joined to ours, provide a practical course of action which will enable the parish to work as a unit, come right out of its shell, and become again a conquering community.

II A LIVING, APOSTOLIC LITURGY

Anyone who assists at services in your church can see that you go to considerable effort to get the people to share in the liturgy. Do you think that the prayers of the people have any great importance, from a missionary viewpoint?

There are tremendously important. The Christian life to which we are trying to attract souls is not, we realize, merely a way to pray; but since it is the life of Christ, and since Christ lived to give praise to the Father, we can say that the Christian way of life is principally a worship of God. Our goal is 'to make our brothers Christian', but it is obvious that they will not suddenly start coming to Mass or to devotions; they will come only by degrees, impelled by the growing conviction that Christianity is a complete way of life. It is only at the last stage that we shall have to worry about assimilating them into the praying, sacrificing Church.

But in the meantime, it is essential that we give these prospective converts the kind of Christian worship that will continue to attract them, that will keep them coming, once the first breach is made in their paganism. Also we must use it to teach them, and draw them gradually along to a full realization of the Christian mysteries.

As a matter of fact, almost the same could be said for the Christians themselves, especially the young ones. If we want to keep them in the Church, we must let them share her life and not be mere spectators. If we want them to become dynamic apostles, our ceremonies must help them to become conscious of the meaning of Christianity.

That is not usually the case.

Unfortunately, it is not. It takes no prolonged survey of our parishes to see that the way in which our ceremonies are usually conducted is far from edifying. More often than not they are boring, empty, meaningless. An unbeliever who went into a Catholic church to see for himself what Catholic services were like would almost certainly come out yawning.

Nevertheless, strenuous efforts are being made to vivify the Liturgy.

Indeed there are, and we are grateful for them. Certainly

we do not think that this book is a pioneer, nor that we are the first ones to set down or to try new ideas. Rather we realize our position as a part of a growing stream, in which we are carried along more by the efforts of contemporary apostles in every line than by our own. The liturgical movement is growing, but it is still too weak, too little understood. Our contribution will try to make it less so.

What are the major weak spots in our Liturgy, such as it is?

The description of a Sunday-morning Mass is the most devastating answer we can think of. Let us take a look at a typical scene.

The Low Mass is going on. A few men are standing up at the back of the church and gazing around. Further up, the church is pretty well filled, with women mostly; some are saying their beads, to the accompaniment of clicking and of audible 'Hail Marys'. Some are reading prayer books or missals. Some are seated while the rest kneel; for no apparent reasons there are periodic reverses of position. Only during the reading of the Gospel is the whole church in the same position. At the altar, the priest moves back and forth, reciting words that no one beyond the front pews can hear; he turns round from time to time for a 'Dominus vobiscum', to which only the altar boy answers. Obviously he is isolated, cut off from the people behind him. Obviously the people in that Church are not a community, but a mere collection of individuals, praying individually as best they can.

At one point contact between priest and people does seem to be made. A priest mounts the pulpit and makes the parish announcements (often poorly read), and talks on various subjects (often on money). Then comes the sermon (of which we have much to say later on), and it seems to be made up of a collection of clichés that are completely foreign to the ordinary, daily problems of this people; anyhow, they have heard them all before.

After the sermon, the Sacrifice begins again, and the collection begins too. Everyone starts looking in their pockets or pocketbooks for their offering, and the ushers give change as they go along. Then, those who are trying to follow the Mass settle back and try to find out where the priest is now.

At the Elevation, a hush comes over the church. Some of the people bow down; others look up at the Host and the Chalice. Immediately afterwards the collection continues, beads start to rattle again, mingled with the sound of turning pages, and so to the Communion.

At the 'Agnus Dei', those who want to receive start towards the altar-rail, and, pretty soon, the aisles are choked with men and women coming and going to and from the rail. Everyone gets back into place, despite the usual lack of co-operation from others in the same pew, and settles back in thanksgiving.

'Ite Missa est', and some are already on their way out to join those who left after the Communion; the better ones wait till the Last Gospel is read. Well, that's over!

We have just assisted at the most solemn act of the Christian community at prayer, the offering of Christ to the Trinity by his Mystical Body, the Church.

At the High Mass, it is a little different. The priest at the altar is more prominent because he is chanting. But the church is only a quarter filled. Present are those who 'must' be there—school children, duly watched over by the nuns, and bored by the whole proceedings; they have to keep quiet, and all in all find the service far from appealing. The nuns are there, partly to watch over the children, and partly to 'give a good example'. The choir is there. Scattered here and there through the church are a few adults. That is the cross-view we get of the parish at the official parish Mass.

The people who are present do not sing at High Mass; they listen. For the most part, they do not understand either the Latin or the meaning of their missal translations; because to understand, they would have to have had explanations and training, and no one has given them that. So they are bored too; bored willingly and without resentment, but still bored.

A proof of this is found in the way our people avoid the High Mass; nobody wants to come to it. Who can blame them? It is difficult for anyone to see in this uncomprehended expression of worship the solemn and official prayer which the Church is rendering to God. It is not the community at prayer. In fact it is even less so than the earlier Low Mass we observed, since few, if any, go to Communion at this one.

Look at the last Mass on Sunday. Liturgical chant has given way to hymns by a soloist or by a choir, or even to musical renderings of a violin or violoncello. The working families have given way to the more prosperous members of the parish, because working people in their less stylish dress would feel out of place in this crowd.

At least they come, and that is something.

What good is it, if we do not get them to pray? Surely we cannot be so blind as to think that the mere material performance of the obligation of Sunday Mass is pleasing to God! Surely we cannot be so legalistic as to think that this is all that the Church wants!

What have you to say about services other than Mass?

Some parishes still keep up the practice of Sunday Vespers, mostly for the principle of the thing; almost no one comes to it. We have processions, too, straggling things that have no other purpose than to let the parish priest feel comforted in seeing his 'parish' around him, and—as Father Ramillieux said, 'to give illusory satisfaction to the Heart of Jesus'. At these things too, our deadly and ever-present enemy—boredom—is present. No one knows quite why he is walking around the church.

Then there are the months of Saint Joseph, of our Lady, of the Sacred Heart, in which the clergy can preside over tiny gatherings of the same faithful souls and at which they can continue giving Benediction of the Blessed Sacrament. No one seems to be any better off for them; at least they do not show any more Christian vitality or apostolicity. Meanwhile, the 'others' are still staying away, because these affairs have no connection with their daily lives.

Is it not strange and sad that we satisfy ourselves with all this, when we could organize ceremonies which would be understood, which would be pointed to the lives of non-Christians, and which would help win them to Christ? Strange and sad, too, is the fact that we seem incapable of opening or closing any service with anything but an 'Our Father' or a 'Hail Mary', which everyone repeats automatically, thoughtlessly. It certainly seems that there is no realization of a community at prayer. Even in the morning or evening prayers that some parishes and schools keep up the words are hurried, the formulas are not understood.

How do you explain all these difficulties in the celebration of Christian worship?

The explanation is simple enough; we have let ourselves fall into a lazy spirit of 'conforming'. We misapply the words of Saint Paul, who told us to guard the deposit of Faith, and we hold on for dear life to traditions. Over and over again we repeat things 'the way they are done in this parish', and make no effort to adapt them to the needs of those who are our parishioners, whom we are neglecting. It seems to be a cherished illusion of us priests that the faithful who are present at services are getting some good from what we give them; in reality, they are politely bored. They shift for themselves, and manage to pray as individuals and in their individual ways. The attendance at ceremonies other than Mass frightens us sometimes, and we make appeals, trying to get more to come, 'to give good example'. Or we try the other approach, and thank those who were good enough to come. The truth is, and we know it, that they will not come in any increasing numbers until we change our methods.

Your criticisms are valid, and most priests will admit that. The question is, what changes can you suggest? How do you manage things in your own parish?

The answer to those questions involves so many factors that we must beg for time to explain. Everything that is done at Colombes flows from these two basic principles. First, that the parish is a community, and its prayer must be communal; second, that our parishioners belong to the working classes, and so our collective prayer must be adapted to their lives. Going one step further, we distinguish two fields of action. The liturgy as it exists now is the prayer of the faithful, and it must be celebrated with the 'Old Christians' in mind, even though we try to think also of the new converts present, and also of the pagans who may, occasionally, be present. On the other hand, there are 'para-liturgical' ceremonies, usually at night, which are

29

pointed directly at those outside the fold, even though Christians, too, may benefit from them.

Permit us to explain the two basic principles we gave above. Our liturgy must be *communal* if it is to be living, apostolic. At first glance, that phrase may seem trite, but yet it is the key to the revolution of the parish. We priests must convince ourselves first of all, and then convince the faithful, that the parish is a unit, a pocket-size edition of the ONE Church. This parish has its prayer and worship to render to God, not as individuals but as a collective and social unit. Church services are meant to be group prayers. Mass in the parish church is the Sacrifice of Christ being offered by this part of his Mystical Body for the whole Body, and there is no place for personal peculiarities of prayer in this act. All this must be meditated upon, explained, repeated, because it is the very cornerstone of our programme; until this is grasped, there can be no further building. No leniency can be allowed for any opposition which would endanger the communal character of parochial prayer; that includes personal, direct opposition by any of the parishioners, and it also includes the type of parishioner who likes to frequent chapels or parish churches other than his or her own. Coupled with that, we must do our best to organize our own ceremonies in the best possible manner. That will be easier in working-class parishes than in ones where wealthier people predominate, because workers are less individualistic and, generally, more co-operative.

The second principle is that the liturgy must be *adapted*. That does not mean discarding canon law, or doing anything contrary to express rubrics; the Church can decide about changes which involve either of the above cases. We limit ourselves to what is here and now permissible, and will give some examples of what we mean later on; for the time being we will explain some of our general principles. As long as Low Masses are celebrated as they now are, our task is to see that the people participate to the utmost, and in a way suited to their mentality; what the priest is doing must become intelligible, and its relation to their lives must become apparent. Instead of this, we see all around us the spectacle of souls left to personal piety, to Rosaries, or to hymns that have little or no connection with the supreme Sacrifice going on before them. The ones who worry about the laxity of ecclesiastical authorities in allowing adaptations aimed at making the liturgy more understandable should rather marvel that the same authorities have done so little to prevent a tragedy such as the above. It seems to us that these 'terrible' adaptations are preferable, by far. In making them we must see that they permeate everything connected with the Church—hymns, prayers, translations. We must see that they mean something to the people for whom they are intended. We must not make them for our own satisfaction, nor to show our powers of expression, nor to show a mirror of our lives. They are the people's, and they are meant to revivify them.

How do you go about applying all this?

The Low Masses celebrated at Colombes are a good example of what we mean; the parish Mass—a High Mass —can be treated later. First of all, a word of warning; we make the Low Masses as *high* as possible. This means that, in accordance with the rubrics, we say everything allowable in a tone which can be heard by everyone. The faithful have a right to hear the Mass, and we have the obligation of ridding ourselves of the habit of mumbling in such a way that the server can hardly hear us. More than that, we have the obligation of letting the people *see* Mass, and of grasping the purpose behind our movements. A young priest remarked once that it was only when he was actually learning how to say Mass himself that he discovered that there were Signs of the Cross made over the chalice at different times; he had served Mass often enough, but he had never realized that the sweeping movements he saw priests making were Signs of the Cross! A good many of the faithful can say the same thing. Our people have learned to answer the prayers of the priest together, to say the Gloria, Credo, Sanctus, Agnus Dei. They have learned to stand together for the Gloria, Credo, Preface and Pater Noster; to sit together for the Epistle and after the Credo; to kneel together from the Sanctus to the Agnus Dei. Before Mass begins we always give an understandable summary of the *Ordo* for the day. A dream which we have not been able to realize yet is to have the Epistle and Gospel, at least, read in the vernacular. Some day that will come, using laymen trained for this purpose.

How well do the people follow these directions?

They are completely co-operative about answering the prayers, but not quite as much so about posture; a few pious souls still insist on kneeling throughout the Mass.

Tell us about the Parish Mass.

Sometimes, but not ordinarily, it is a High Mass. We are of the opinion that High Masses should be chanted by the entire congregation, and, until that day can come, we are sparing of them. If they are chanted by a choir or a *schola*, the faithful become mere spectators, and that is not the purpose of the liturgy. In a mission parish like ours we cannot do all the things that a completely Christian one can. High Masses will come gradually.

Here at Colombes the parish Mass is at eight o'clock so that the faithful may receive Communion at it. We try to have the whole parish proportionately represented—youths, adults, parents. All the priests are on hand, to greet and seat the arrivals. There are no reserved seats; the first to come fill up the front of the church, and so on till it is full. Every pew has the same type of missal in it, and the people leave them there after Mass; they can own a copy if they wish, but every other type of missal or prayer-book is mercilessly prohibited. The reason for this is so that all may be together, page by page.

Our people have become an active community when at Mass through their collective responses to the prayers. Mass is followed attentively, and what was once a serious innovation has become the accepted thing. In addition to the responses in Latin, sometimes there are prayers or hymns expressive of the different parts of the Mass. We have no regular *schola* (choir); the .whole congregation takes up the prayers and hymns with their priests in their midst.

Quite often Mass is celebrated on an altar which has been moved out near the congregation. On the big feast days it is set up on a platform in the middle of the Church. These occasions are still the exceptions, and Mass is usually said in the usual place. On Sunday the bread and wine are placed on a table in the body of the church, and at the Offertory the priest brings them to the altar as a more obvious symbol of the fact that they are the offerings of the people.

What about collections?

The collection, please, for we have only one. Payment of pew rent has been replaced by a quarterly donation which is given when the people are leaving the Church. The regular Sunday collection is taken with a minimum of distraction by the priests or laymen during the Credo. It is over by the time the Offertory ends.

Do you have any special ceremonies for the major feasts?

Here again we try to adapt according to the conditions we face. You have doubtless noticed that the Holy Week ceremonies are more mysterious and removed from the people than is the ordinary liturgy; that is because the liturgy itself was made up when all work was halted for a week, so that everyone could concentrate on worship, but the pattern of life has changed, and we are in a mission land.

What a chance these days are to announce Christ to our people! What beauty and solemnity in these feast-days! As far as the Church is concerned, they should be as they always have been—the most moving, the most welcome days, and we have tried to keep this note in any adaptations we made.

Since we were just talking about collections, we should like to emphasize the fact that we never take one on days like these. It works to our advantage, from an apologetic angle, and it is a real aid to the devotion of the faithful.

On Palm Sunday it is wise to do something which will make an appeal to as many as possible, because many of those at church on that one day are just the ones we want to win over. The ceremonies have to make an impression; the triumph of Christ must be portrayed. We cannot afford to let this day be merely one when palms are to be brought home for cemetery decorations, or for good-luck charms. So we have adapted and translated almost all the liturgical texts which the congregation is supposed to say or sing.

Naturally, we have kept the official services of Holy

Week, but because their very length makes them impossible for most to attend, we thought it wise to give an explanation of them at evening services. We have symbolic representations of the next day's Gospel performed by the young people, translated hymns sung to gregorian chant by the whole congregation, choirs to say the prayers adapted from the liturgy of Good Friday, translations of the Reproaches (which have become almost meaningless to the majority, because of their lack of Biblical knowledge). The result of all this has been that, besides the fifty or sixty adults present for the morning Masses, we have been able to get five or six hundred to pray at night during Holy Week.

At the parish Mass on Easter Sunday we have a ceremony based on the blessing of the new fire, while the 'Exsultet' is sung in French. We have tremendous crowds at this service, whereas there is but a handful present on Holy Saturday morning. After all, our people have to work for a living. In 1945, despite the fact that we are in a pagan district, there were 1400 at church on Easter Sunday and 1250 of them went to Communion.

For Christmas we utilized a long-standing custom here, and put on a real Christmas Eve celebration, with old carols and plays, and a good crowd turned out for that. A large number of those present were ones we wanted to convert, and the good feeling caused by the party did much to put them in the proper frame of mind for the Midnight Mass which followed. In 1944 we used a choir which portrayed four scenes: 'The world needs a Saviour' (in our homes, our work, our hearts); 'The Saviour is born' (carols); 'Those who welcomed Christ' (the people, shepherds, workers). All of these take place on a raised platform, where Mass is then celebrated. The success of this venture was encouraging; about 1800 persons stayed for the whole ceremony, and many of them were certainly not church-goers.

I understand that you have special ceremonies for some new feasts?

Yes, we use them to bring out the point of a sermon, or to support some programme we have under way, or to capitalize on some legal holiday, or for a representation of a liturgical season.

For example we decided to profit by the popularity of a Mothers' Day, so as to sanctify it and recall its meaning to families. So, for that day, we reserve the main aisle for mothers; a cradle is set up towards the front of the Church, as a symbol of their devotion and their maternity. At the Offertory, the mothers come up, and have photographs of their children placed on the altar. In the afternoon, we bless the cradle and the mothers at Benediction; and after this very moving ceremony the children bring to their mothers the magnificent bunches of flowers they have been carrying before the Host. We also have a feast called 'The Christian Joys of Mothers'. For this there is also an afternoon service, with a choir chanting a special 'Litany of the Family'; during this there is a procession of young mothers with their newly-baptized children in their arms, then the first communicants, followed by young men who have just become engaged, carrying their engagement gift for their fiancées. Bringing up the rear is a young priest, accompanied by his old mother. The ceremony concludes with the blessing of the new priest, first to his own mother, and then to all.

To bring home our preaching, we also organized a 'Feast of the Gospel', preparing for it by plenty of propaganda about reading the New Testament and by instruction on this subject in the catechism classes. For the feast itself the church was decorated with symbols of the evangelists and with murals depicting scenes in the life of Christ. The Gospel of the day was chanted with special solemnity. At night a deacon chanted answers taken from the Gospels in response to the terrible questions of our own times; a good crowd was present—and most of them were unbelievers.

In the same way a 'Feast of the Mass' was used to illustrate and clarify a series of sermons on the Mass, and also to help make clear our constant effort to make the Mass 'everybody's Mass'. As a crowded church watched, men of the parish brought forward three benches; these were to be the altar. An altar boy carried in the altar stone. Skilled and willing hands had made the crucifix, candelabra, the altar cloths and vestments, and even had written and designed the missal. As all these were brought forward, a priest in the pulpit described each article. To make the Mass more personal, everyone brought up, at the Offertory, an envelope containing a list of his or her own special intentions. The children each bring up a piece of coloured glass; when the pieces are fitted together, the phrase 'The Mass is the centre of our lives' is spelt out. As each child comes up with his piece, he says aloud, 'This is to make my Mass mean more'. The evening service is used to develop the same idea. Up to the altar are brought the tools of the workmen, household objects, school-books, children's games, and bread and wine. Meanwhile a long chanted prayer fits all these things into the harmony of Christian living and unites all the crowd in an inspiring prayer. The ceremony closes with veneration of the altar-stone.

In a more or less similar fashion we have started a feast of the Missions, of the Cross (during Lent), of the Apostolate (with a blessing of the parish quarters and a development of our plan of conquest), of Baptism (together with the baptism of a group of elder children), of Catechism, etc. We are not saying that every parish priest should do all this, but we are pleased that many priests asked us to compile a handbook of such ceremonies.

We insist on the necessity of creating and developing a catechumen-directed liturgy which will not supplant our traditional liturgy, but yet which will be useful in evangelizing a people who are woefully ignorant and who learn more from participation than from listening. It amounts to a use of the modern ideas on 'active educational methods' among people who are only children so far as religious knowledge is concerned.

Have you done anything like the above for Baptism, Funerals, etc.?

From a missionary angle these services present the best opportunity to us, because of the presence of so many persons who, ordinarily, never come near a church. We all know how ceremonies like these are so often hurried through, and how the group concerned stands around, laughing and whispering—totally unconscious of the tremendous mystery taking place before them. At Baptisms, the only time they crane forward to look is when the priest puts the salt on the baby's tongue. At marriages, the only interesting thing is the costume of the bride. Even funerals—which could be such a marvellous occasion for touching the hearts of the people—remain cold and meaningless to our people. Surely there is nothing to prevent us making these important Christian ceremonies *live*, and using them as powerful tools of evangelization.

At our place everyone who assists at a Baptism uses a leaflet in which are translations of all the prayers and simple explanations of the whole service. One priest performs the rite, and another one describes each step; in this way it becomes clear that here we have the gateway into Christianity, the mystery of incorporation into Christ. We use this opportunity to remind the parents of the obligation of a Christian upbringing for this child. The liturgical Pastoral of Vanves (January 1945) expresses a splendid proposal of having collective Baptisms every Sunday, publicized so that a good crowd will attend. Honestly, it is hard to understand how this most important Sacrament—the one by which the Christian community grows—has come to be an individual, almost clandestine, ceremony. It used to be a communal act. The very purpose of Lent is a public retreat for all these preparing to receive Baptism. Since we are again a mission land, it certainly seems possible to bring back this idea to our own times, at least to some extent.

Class-distinctions must be a big obstacle for you at marriages.

Not at all. While it is true that we have not officially done away with these 'classes', we still avoid them. When anyone comes to arrange for a marriage, and mentions 'money', we answer 'sacrament', 'prayer', 'preparation for marriage' until they get the idea that money does not interest us and that the stipend will be normal. If they insist, and demand the frills which involve expense, we give in, but such a case, however, occurs not more than once a month. We think that the best way to discourage these class distinctions is to restore, with all possible religious solemnity, the liturgy of the nuptial Mass and to have the whole congregation pray at it. In this way the 'smartest' marriage will be that at which the people prayed with the greatest devotion, namely the marriage of good Christians, whose many friends prayed wholeheartedly during the Mass. We have a leaflet for use at weddings; in it are all the words and prayers of the Nuptial Mass in French, together with the text of the Blessing and various other prayers made up for the occasion. As at Baptism, a second priest explains the ceremony and leads the people. Experience shows us that friends of the young couple are more than willing to say these prayers, and the custom of receiving Communion at the wedding Mass is becoming more common. In such cases, the bride and groom bring up the host and the wine, while each of the other participants brings a small host. We never neglect a chance to speak about the Christian ideal of marriage and of the family during the customary brief sermon. Besides weddings, we have also celebrated Engagement Masses, with adapted prayers and chant.

What do you do at funerals?

They are one of our best opportunities to reach the people. When we think of pastors who organize celebrations in the parish hall, just to be able to say a little bit about religion to those who never come to church, we are astounded that they should miss their chance at funerals—when the same type of person is sure to be present. At such times, these are sure to be better prepared to listen to teachings on religion than they would be at some parish hall 'get-together'. Why not make the most of it then?

Some do, but only to utter some general exhortations, or to praise the deceased. We let the liturgy give the sermon. When the body is met at the church, the celebrant gives a brief outline of the ceremony and its lesson on eternity; then everyone is invited to pray for the dead person, using the leaflet provided and its rhymed translation of the De Profundis. During the Mass another priest reads the translated Introit, Collect, Epistle (itself a good sermon), etc. All recite the Pater Noster. Chants are used too; for example, the paraphrased Kyrie of the Requiem Mass. At the Absolution, some of the prayers are said in the vernacular. When a whole group of families is seen in this sort of prayer, the effect is moving. More than that, the scene itself preaches a sermon which no one can ignore.

38

Many have come back to God because of it.

It is easy to see that the distinction of 'classes' no longer seems so important, with funerals like these. The emphasis is shifted from the organ and the decorations to the expression of a common heartfelt prayer. A typical expression of how our people feel is found in what one of my parishioners told me: 'I was at a fourth-class funeral in Paris the other day. Can you imagine? They didn't even have a prayer-leaflet in the seats, nor any priest to lead the people in prayer!'

When the funerals take place in the afternoon (as about half do), we begin as we do in a morning service at the meeting of the body; then the Epistle is read because of its tremendous lesson; some paraphrased Psalms or liturgical prayers are then chanted, and we finish with the absolution. We announce a Mass on the following day for the soul of the deceased, because we always celebrate a Mass for every deceased member of our parish.

From all you have said, it seems that you have very little confidence in the liturgy as it is, in Latin Gregorian chant, etc.?

The answer, as always, is that we are in a mission land. We could, of course, adapt the liturgy in a strictly traditional sense; that would be even easier for us. We could certainly find some young people who would be willing to take a course in gregorian chant and form a *schola*. Under a musically-minded curate (who would probably be changed in a few years) we could have fine liturgical chant, to tickle our aesthetic ears. We might even reach the point of having the whole congregation sing at High Mass, as we actually do sometimes. We could do all this—but we should be missing our goal. We should satisfy the little group of the faithful, but we should leave everyone else as indifferent as they now are; we should be limiting still further the deadly parish atmosphere. If we were dealing with completely Christian parishes, then we should do all these things. Look at it from the mission viewpoint, and see if such a procedure would make for growth, or for stagnation. Our job, like that of most parishes in this year of Our Lord 1945, is very different. Our people have everything to learn. We think (and shall develop this idea under the heading of

'Culture'), that our people can be influenced only by community action, by which they can *live* their praise of God, and *live* the life of Christ. After all, what is the liturgy, but the collective life of the whole Christian community 'through Christ, with Christ and in Christ', directed towards the Father? If we can realize this, we are fulfilling our task, provided we really reach this end.

All our liturgical efforts are meant to form a warm, living, dynamic community. We are building neither an ivory tower nor a monastery but an active community which will attract others because they find it attractive, which will stimulate its members because it is alive.

You have mentioned chants and hymns quite often. I should imagine that you would not care too much for such things.

We realize that the word 'chant' or 'hymn' has a bad connotation. We often hear people regretting the passing of the 'good old hymns', even though most of them are products of the last century. Most of them are trash, with words so sweet and sickly that we would be ashamed to ask normal adults to sing them; even the melodies are generally affected and dreamy. Look through a hymn-book and criticize its contents from the triple viewpoint of doctrine, taste and realism; see how many will pass this test. To call Our Lady 'O, Our Only Hope' is a terrible exaggeration, for that title is Christ's. To use phrases like 'Languid Glances' is mawkish. To call Jesus in the Tabernacle the 'Divine Captive' is heresy. To ask anyone to sing after Communion 'O, Ineffable Sweetness', or 'I Taste the Sweetness of Holy Love' is to ask of them what a saint might feel once in a lifetime. Certainly it does not correspond to the feeling of most communicants, and it only serves to make them think that they are not as they should be. That is wrong! Furthermore, we should not insist on expressions like 'Christians, Raise Your Banners!', because they do nothing but cause laughter.

But that is not the worst part of it. The really regrettable thing is that we are making the people use words which are meaningless. They certainly do not profit much from using words like 'Cherubim', 'the Sanctuary', 'a holy transport', 'a transgression', 'a foretaste of heavenly joys' or

a 'safe haven'. All these words are in the dictionary, but
not in their vocabulary. Consequently, they connect these
words with unearthly, illusory things—and that is what
does harm. Because these hymns do not sound true, because
they cannot feel these sentiments, because they express
things completely foreign to life, it too often follows that the
religion which uses them must also be untrue, unfelt,
foreign. Too often that very conclusion is reached by many
an adult whom we have brought up on such stuff. We
only hope that teachers and priests will notice this.

Equally false is the longing for heaven which we try to
make our people express, when they know only the things
of earth. 'Oh, how bitter and tasteless to me are earthly
joys!' 'Would that I could fly like a fugitive dove to heaven!'
The notion that the service of God brings nothing but joy
is almost as bad: 'Let me always taste Thy secret sweetness',
or 'All sadness turns to Joy in Thee'.

We firmly believe in a merciless eradication of such un-
healthy, unsafe hymns. When we talk about hymns at
Colombes, as you remarked, you can be sure that they are
not like any of the above examples. It certainly is possible
to compose splendid vernacular hymns, with words that are
simple and prayerful, with tunes that are neither dances,
marches nor wails. We could mention a few that we had
made up over the last five years, but we do not wish to set
them up as models. We tried to express real Christian
sentiments in words that can be understood; anyone can
do as much. They are powerful and moving, when a whole
church is singing the liturgy of a particular ceremony in
terms that are exact, and yet familiar. In this sense, then,
we do believe in the use of hymns.

*Do you think that we should do away with Latin and Gregorian
chant?*

Never! Latin must remain the liturgical language, for
several reasons. The liturgy is the prayer of the Universal
Church, and it is good to pray in the same tongue that our
brothers of old used, and our brothers throughout the world
still use. Also, Latin, because it is beyond the stage of
change, serves as a fine basis for varying modern translations. If we had a French liturgy based on the language

spoken in the days of Froissart, it would be incomprehensible by now and would need translation as much as Latin does; there would be a constant necessity of bringing such liturgy up to date. For example, read some of the prayers which Fénélon wrote for use at Mass, and see how unintelligible they are now. Experience proves that real Christians, and converts too, once they are integrated into Catholic life, find no repugnance in the use of Latin, as long as good translations are available. When we say 'good' translations, we do not mean transliterations, because such are as mysterious as Latin itself. There is no point in translating 'qui sedes super Cherubim' into 'Who sittest above the Cherubim'. What we need are translations which keep the Latin sense and still mean something to the ordinary people who read little more than the newspaper. That is not easy to do; we know, because we have tried. But it is absolutely necessary. If we have such translations, our people can easily sing or say parts of the Latin ordinary of the Mass, and easily follow the rest of it. In time, the people can even sing some of the better known gregorian melodies.

So—for the Christian community, Latin which is well translated, adapted, together with some vernacular ceremonies; also gregorian chant, but together with some vernacular music. But, for the pagans, French that is modern and yet keeps the spirit of the liturgy, without symbolisms which would not be understood anyway.

Do you not find that the different levels of society and of culture among the people make a real difficulty?

No, because in a parish like ours we deliberately try to create a workers' atmosphere. Now that may be surprising, because the church should seem to be hospitable to all classes, without any distinctions. At Colombes we began, five years ago, to stress what would appeal to the working class, even though, now, you would not especially notice any such emphasis. We had to, because it was necessary to put the workers at ease in the church, and also to rid them of the notion that religion was 'a middle-class affair'; moreover, if we expected them to make prayer a living part of their lives and sorrows and joys and needs, we had to bring in references to their factories and work and homes.

42

In a working-class parish you must use working-class language.

Likewise the people ought to be able to find things with which they are acquainted, in the decorations of the church, in the feasts we made up. Naturally there can never be a question of admitting the use of anything that is trite or in bad taste.

What do your other parishioners—the lawyers, doctors, and the like—say about all this?

Some protested, and some still do, but it is because they still do not understand. What can we do? We are so sure that we have to take a firm stand. By leaning a little more to the workers' side we know that we can bring back the balance which should be in our community.

Gradually the ice of our stiff middle-class is breaking, their formalism is bending, and we do not have to insist as much as we used to on the working-class direction of our common prayer. Once a worker feels 'at home', feels wanted and loved, the need of such insistence on our part disappears. Little by little the balance comes back, and all can pray together.

What do you think of the use of children's choirs?

For one thing, we are sick of hearing people tell us things like this: 'Oh, I used to love the prayers and the ceremonies; you see, I was a member of the choir until I was seventeen years old'. Every priest has heard this sort of thing a hundred times—often from those who are bitter opponents of the Church.

Because that is so often the case we ought to think a bit. If the result of organizing children into a choir is going to be adult apostasy, we would rather not have anything to do with it. We realize that many apostates use their childhood memories as a mere cloak to hide the real reasons why they left the Church, but we do not want to provide even the cloak.

One of the chief reasons for this unfriendly attitude is that, too often, we pick only the 'good' children for our organizations. Too often, the ones we pick are those who seem incapable of anything very bad—or very good, either; they are dead-heads, as far as the other children are concerned. We were speaking like this to a fellow priest one day, and he was cynical enough to answer: 'True enough, but our prospective vocations come from them'. That must not be! The members of the choir must not be 'little saints' and 'sissies', a 'culture' in which we find vocations. We have had fifteen members of the parish enter the minor Seminary in the last five years (not to mention the belated vocations to the Major Seminary), and these fifteen were *not* grown-up choir boys of that type.

It is easy to make a closed group, a little caste, out of the altar boys or choir; easy, because the fact that they have been specially picked, have special meetings, have special knowledge of the rites and the Latin, tends to set them apart and above the ordinary Catholic. We must not let this happen. Nothing does more to take possible apostles out of their own environment; nothing does more harm to their sense of conquest for the cause of Christ. It may make us feel good to see children who know the ceremonies of Holy Week inside out, who know all about High Masses, even Pontifical Masses—but what good does it do *them?* What good will that sort of knowledge be in their lives as workers? What good will it do for the prayer life of the family to be founded one day by these young Christians? We have given them an ecclesiastical tinge, and nothing more. After all, it takes but an average memory and but ordinary poise to sing or serve at Mass. It takes much more to get in with one's fellow-workers at the shop, so as to win them over to Christ. That is the hard task, and a thankless, often unsuccessful one. Consequently, if the only special service we demand of the talent of our youth is a little memorizing of words and gestures and the necessity of showing up for different functions, we cannot blame them for stopping there. We cannot blame them for losing their apostolic zeal.

Aren't you exaggerating?

We wish we were. Let us give you but one example of what we mean.

In our parish (and remember that we are deliberately a mission-minded parish), we put a layman in charge of the altar-boys, to train them in Latin, ceremonies and general smoothness. It seems that this layman went a little beyond our commission, and he gave the boys a real course in liturgical functions. Still, what harm in that? However, one day, when we had planned to have a High Mass for some special feast, something happened, and we decided to have a Dialogue Mass instead. Do you know what the result of that was? Our altar boys were peeved, and said that they would not serve any more in a parish that had so few Solemn Masses! We had a job on our hands trying to convince them that it was a case of the general good, that we were a mission parish, etc. It did not seem to matter to them that we had to have a general policy of adaptation according to the needs of our parishioners, that there were souls to save, that everyone had to make sacrifices of personal tastes in order to bring Christ to the parish. Only one thing mattered to them; they had taken the trouble of learning the ceremonies of High Mass and they wanted to put them to use. Their satisfaction came first; that was that.

What do you suggest then—do away with Choir and Altar Societies?

No; after all, we do have to have ceremonies. We should, however, think of the souls of these children rather than consider their usefulness to us. We should not have the same one serving two or three Masses in succession, for example.

A better system is that at Notre Dame d'Espérance, where they have no special groups for the choir or for serving Mass. Every boy of the parish is invited to serve, and the system is succeeding so well that the poor priest is forced to make a choice of candidates thronging around him before every Mass; he looks over the eager faces and the outstretched arms and picks out the one who seems best-disposed and most worthy on that particular day. In this way no élite is set up, no break is made between servers and non-servers, and much of the formalism which can affect altarboys is avoided.

We should be able to see that many young workers have no liking for ceremonies. We should realize that putting on a cassock and surplice compromises a young man—even a Jocist—in the eyes of his companions. Such an attitude

45

is understandable, and should not make priests resentful, rather, it should make us discreet about whom we ask and how and where. Some will serve Mass, but grudgingly and merely because we asked them; others will do so willingly, but without realizing that it may be unwise for them. We want to preserve their influence; we should not risk their losing it.

By way of conclusion to these ideas on the liturgy, we should like to point out that, while this subject is an important one, it is by no means the most important part of our concept of a mission parish. We say this because many priests—to judge from their conversation when they come here for a visit—seem to think that the liturgy holds the answer for any and every pastoral problem.

We wish that it could be as easy as all that! It is vital that our Christian communities be given a real and communal spiritual life, but liturgical adaptation is but one among many answers to the many evils which we are facing. Seeing the wretched condition of so many souls, we are driven further by our zeal for conquest, and we must find ways that will be even more useful, even if more difficult to put into practice, and these, in turn, will intensify the common life of prayer of our people.

III A MISSIONARY APOSTOLATE

I. THE PROBLEM OF ACTIVITIES

It is, of course, important to restore or re-establish a living liturgy for the sake of the apostolate, since we want to be able to offer to new converts a form of worship which will attract them and show them the way to God. But our first problem is more fundamental, because these converts must first come to church before they can share in its liturgy. And they must be contacted before they can be converted. What approaches do you have in mind for that?

We agree that this is the fundamental problem. It is also a very difficult one, and one requiring a great deal of discussion.

First of all, we ought to look at what has been done in this field.

Over the last hundred years a vast amount of energy has been expended in this apostolic task, and has been expended with devotion, zeal and intelligence, as anyone who made a study of our parishes would admit. Usually we lump all these varied forms of apostolic energy under the classification of 'activities' (Oeuvres). The Church in France, especially since she realized the spread and might of the de-Christianizing forces, has set up a network of activities in almost every parish, and this has done much for the vitality of individual parishes. So much so that when a priest says that he has flourishing parish societies, he is equivalently saying that his parish is active, and that he and the curates are kept busy. Looking back on the parish of former years, when priests were more numerous, one cannot help but wonder what priests did with their time in those days, and what contact they had with non-Catholics. Nowadays it is practically impossible to conceive of a parish without also thinking of its many and varied societies. Priests who ought to know say that these are the mainstays of parish life.

Is that your opinion too?

For the moment it is, because doing away with such activities would mean, in most parishes, the end of any

47

apostolic endeavour. Here, in this chapter, we are not advocating their suppression, and we ask the reader not to misunderstand us on this point. We want to outline all the good factors of these activities—not with the malicious intent of making later criticism more telling—but wanting honestly to see good where there is good.

The danger in them is a real one, because they are so integral a part of parish life that they tend to submerge us in a round of activity which we no longer stop to analyse and appreciate correctly. We are like workmen who are so busy using their tools that they will not stop to sharpen and align them. In the years that we have lived as curate and pastor, we noticed certain defects and shortcomings, and we should like to point them out now.

For a beginning, would you say that some line of demarcation must be drawn? We lump too many things under this vague title of 'Activities'—everything from recreational projects to the Jocists. Maybe we should be more scientific, and limit the extension of the term.

Absolutely. Otherwise we shall seem to be criticizing things we do not intend to include. When we talk about 'activities', we certainly do not mean specialized Catholic Action groups, like the Jocists, despite the inability of some priests to see the difference. They add the Jocist Movement to the already large number of parish societies, and see no incongruity in such an attitude. Later on more will be said about these distinct movements, such as the Jocists, the Catholic Trade Unions, which are professional and not parochial, and hence, should not be so classified.

What we do mean by this term are the institutions which have grown up, in and around the church, for the education of our children and young people—recreational centres, parochial summer camps, Scouts and Guides, parish athletic teams, choral groups, etc., etc. Also we mean the charitable endeavours as exemplified by the St Vincent de Paul Society, by soup kitchens, nurseries and the like. Last of all, we include propaganda activity, such as the parish bulletin or plays.

You have mentioned so many and such varied things that it is going to be difficult to analyse them.

We will treat them separately, but a general consideration

makes for a logical beginning. Everyone knows what all these activities have done for the 'restoration' of the Church in France, especially since the separation of Church and State. Everyone admits that they have stirred up the flame of Catholicism, united priests and people, and manifested the life of the Church to an indifferent world.

Where parish activities are well organized, the faithful can satisfy almost all their wants within the parish boundaries. Children come there to play; older boys and girls for their sports and music. The whole family can relax at parish plays or cinema shows, the men have their card games, there is a library, the poor are helped, the sick cared for. No wonder, then, that this complex activity gives the impression of strength and vitality, and that it brings satisfaction to the hearts of priest and people alike. Truly, all these activities are the mainstays of the parish, and we cannot imagine what would happen if they were not there.

Does it seem to you that activities which are so complex will result in completely absorbing the Priests' time and the parish's resources?

It certainly is true that they cost a great deal, in time, in strength and in money; as a matter of fact, it would be true to say that they will consume as much as we are willing to put into them. Think of how much it costs to put up the necessary buildings, to keep them in repair, to engage the necessary staff, etc., etc.! Once a priest has become involved in this sort of thing, he might as well be prepared to face continual worries about money, about organizing all sorts of things to support his plant, about bazaars and raffles. The sermons that he preaches will reflect this preoccupation.

If he should be so fortunate as to get all that he needs, his worries are still not over, because success itself lures him on, with dreams of bigger and better and still more activities. The plans and schemes and ideas become even more complex, and he is caught up in a round of more plans, more financing, more administrative work. What was intended as a means has become an end. Worse still, these activities are a terrible drain on his priestly abilities. Ask any priest how much time he has to spend on organizing and running his programmes, the purely material side of his parish. The answer will show you that practically all his time and energy are being consumed by one phase; very little is left for the other.

True enough, the results are not small. He has, by almost herculean effort, bridged some of the gap between priest and people. The cassocked figure of the priest has been seen often and almost everywhere, and a certain amount of sympathy and understanding has been won. People have come to see that a priest's life is not such an easy one; they have grown from active hostility towards priests to a sort of kindly indifference—if that is a good result. The network of co-ordinated Church programmes has even given us a national prestige; even anti-clerical governments have had to admit that the Church was a living, progressive actuality. The influence of our activities has gone out to those not of the Faith, and has, over the past forty years, contributed much to the training of a youth which has been subjected to some degree of Catholic training. Better still, it has been the cause and occasion of a spiritual élite, separated and moulded to think and live as Christ would have us do. Thousands upon thousands of young men and women have, thanks to these activities, known what it was to talk to a priest, and to receive spiritual direction, such as they never would have gained from any number of Sunday sermons. Much of the vitality of certain parishes, much of the close relationship of priest and people is due to this same influence. It has done much to keep by our side 'tomorrow's generation'.

Everyone agrees about the good results of these activities. What about the often unseen dangers in them which you mentioned a while ago?

In apostolic, as well as military strategy, it is most important not to deceive oneself. Marshal Foch used to say that he wanted to hear the truth and not just favourable reports. We must not be content to maintain, but also to examine, our position. In the light of present conditions there is no place for us priests to applaud one another for the great good we have done, nor to congratulate one another over the Church we have helped build in France.

What we want to say, we shall try to say simply. We are going to tell the results of personal observations, and try to reason back from them to reasons for failures or thwarted advances. All we ask is that no reader should see in our remarks a prejudiced view of any particular activity or person.

All the oratorical precautions that you are taking seem to indicate that this must be a very delicate subject.

Like anything else, it is capable of quiet discussion or of heated argument. We want to avoid the latter, and at the same time avoid a vain and empty discussion, such as in political analyses in the papers. Our purpose is to inspect what has been done—not so much to point out defects as to adapt the methods to changing needs.

Since we are talking about things as complex and elusive as the affairs of everyday life, we do not hope to mark out a complete, all-inclusive programme. Even the maximum that our efforts might attain will affect but a small part of the evil to be overcome. Anyone who opens a debate on the subject of 'methods' simply to force everyone else to accept 'my' method can be certain of a sterile, useless, possibly dangerous discussion.

It is always difficult for anyone who has given himself, heart and soul, to any particular activity and who has known hours of sweet consolation from it, to stand back and force himself to make a cold and rigid examination of his cherished project. Why risk discouragement by looking at its shortcomings, when we know that it is doing some good? How can a man of action find the time or the patience necessary for such investigation? Plenty of people are more than willing to cool our ardour, to cast suspicion on the way we are doing things, without our doing it ourselves. This explains why directors of activities are so notoriously hostile to 'new' methods or 'new' ideas. It explains why parish priests often expect their curates to use the same approach which they themselves used when they were curates. We are not saying that they should not be wary of any sudden and radical changes, or of the inexperience of young priests who like nothing better than change, and who destroy before they know how or what to rebuild. Our point is that there exists a tendency to become afraid, actually afraid, of initiative. Curates will tell you that they dread getting a parish priest who has some pet work which has succeeded, because they will be expected to use no other method than his. He was a revolutionary twenty years ago, but not now! There is a great deal of truth in this sarcasm. If we would only remember that generation succeeds generation in an ever-increasing tempo, especially in our times; needs and conditions are constantly changing. What was successful twenty years ago is not necessarily so to-day. A blindness to that fact accounts for parish priests making their curates endure the same rebuffs that they experienced when they, as young priests, dreamed dreams and saw visions.

Despite all that, we still should be able to reach an objective judgment on this question of activities and methods.

The human factor we spoke of in the previous paragraph is an important one, unfortunately, but there is a more concrete one to be examined. This one is even more harmful to a priest's perspective. Usually it takes the form of one of two tendencies in the apostolate; we either become 'saviours of souls' or 'builders of Christianity'. We shall try to explain what we mean.

The first group sees the salvation of individual souls as the most important goal, and it uses whatever means it may to ensure its contact with young and old. The thing that matters is the number of souls saved on the Last Day. Fish with nets or fish with a line, provided the maximum catch is made for Heaven. The tormenting, saddening, sobering fact is that so many will not be caught, so many are swimming towards eternal ruin.

The others see the validity of this first viewpoint, but they are more disturbed and haunted by the thought of the 'Kingdom of God', which must come. They are more communal in their thought, and their solicitude is directed more towards affecting in some way society as a whole.

In practice, it seems that both viewpoints reach the same end.

Not at all. Each sees the same goal, and no true apostle can exclude either aspect, even though his preference may bend him towards one or the other approach, but there is a difference.

Explain what you mean by this, as regards parochial activities.

If I am preoccupied by the salvation of individual souls, it is clear enough that I will try to attract as many of the faithful as possible by the activities I sponsor. I will want to have as many children and young folk as I can, in catechism classes and recreation periods. I will want to kindle at least a tiny flame of truth in the greatest possible number of my people. If critics want to say that these young people will leave me soon and end up as indifferent Catholics, I say that even the indifferent ones will keep at least a tinge of Christianity from their youthful contact with us, and, some day, they will come home again. Maybe it will be at the hour of death, but they will come back. What can we say to such priestly solicitude? It is a tender, moving thing to see, and we take no pleasure in the criticism we are going to make of it later on.

The other group, the builders of Christianity, does not look at the numbers engaged by our activities, nor does it find such consolation in the semi-indifferent product it sees coming from them. According to this second perspective, society is not a mere mass of individuals, but an organism which requires institutions and leaders; and Christianity itself is something more than a mere ticket to salvation. God's plan for our salvation is built on the nature he gave us, rooted on the humanity with which he created us. Consequently, if some souls can be saved to-day in this pagan society, then many more can be saved tomorrow in a Christian one. This plan says that we must build for the future, even though our work will take years upon years.

In any case, we need not discard one viewpoint for the other; they are not mutually exclusive. But, as Abbé Godin formulated it, the mass of men think as a group, and they will be converted only as a group. We favour this attitude, and will adapt it for our criticism of activities.

Are you saying that these are practically useless for individual conversions?

We are not. Over and over again we have met—or 'reclaimed'—souls who were approachable simply and solely because they had been altar-boys, or had been in some parish society as children. We should be the last to scoff at the value of such contacts.

That is why this chapter intends only to present one phase of a much bigger problem; neither here nor elsewhere do we pretend to be giving solutions. We are looking for them, just as many others are, and we shall keep on looking. At the beginning of this book we said that our only purpose was to evoke interest and provoke thought on all these problems, and such remains our purpose.

Our aim is only to establish a 'mission parish' among 'ordinary' people. From this point of view we are going to criticize parish activities, because we think that too much emphasis has been placed on them, that they have been expected to produce more than they can produce. We should like to see an end to such complete dependence upon them, and an end to the purpose they seem to have, namely, the attracting and keeping of persons who already go to church. We are afraid that they have grown to be obstacles, and not aids, to the apostolate. That is the problem.

It is about time that you began your criticism.

All right, we shall. For the purpose of discussion we are going to group our thoughts under three headings:

1. Recreational activities
2. Educational activities
3. Charitable activities.

RECREATIONAL ACTIVITIES

What do you include under this heading?

Especially all athletic and gymnastic teams, but also any activity which has no other purpose than the occupation of children's leisure time; in other words, anything which amounts to a 'nursery' for boys and girls of varying ages. What we say here will apply, in varying degree, to any other project which, even though it may not have this end in view, obtains the same result.

It is just as well to admit at the outset that we are going to be very hard on these purely recreational groups. In a country parish, or in one where Christianity was flowering, a priest would be wise to organize his young people in this way; in the old days of anti-clericalism they probably served a good purpose, because they brought priest and people together. But here and now, in our day, Catholic Action

54

is the answer to modern needs, and we find it hard to see how a priest who is hard pressed for time in our huge city parishes can give so much of his energy to athletics. At our parish we did away with them, because we had seen the meagre results they bring and the great amount of time and work they consume; judging by our experience, the return on such an investment was not proportionate. Moreover, they do not seem to be apostolic. Sad to say, they even seem to harm, sometimes, the very ones we are trying to help.

I remember one Sunday when our parish teams won many of the events at a field day. I had not seen one of them at Mass that morning, but they were there in full strength that afternoon. When the games were over, one of them said to me: 'You should be proud to be the head of our club, Father. We won everything'. 'Proud? I feel more like crying.'

All the priests with whom we have talked on this subject have seen the same results and come to the same conclusion.

Is it really so difficult to explain these facts? It seems that we are in error, when, in this age of materialism, we foster the cult of muscles and physical strength.

Do not misunderstand. We are not condemning sports or athletics in themselves; we are disgusted with sports that pretend to be 'religious', or claim to be good religious propaganda. Whether we intend it so or not, many a youth who comes to our gyms or games-fields thinks that he is taking part in something religious.

I recall a man telling me one day, after one of the parish teams had been poorly represented numerically at some game, that I spent too much time on non-athletic activities, that I should get more of the young men into the teams. He reasoned that, if a fellow joined a parish team, it was a sign that he was a pretty good Catholic, and that I was foolish to be using other approaches.

Actually a great many young men think that way. If they kick a 'Catholic' football, or hit a 'Catholic' tennis-ball, they are serving the cause of Catholicism; if they win a game, the Church is advancing.

Oh, I know. You will say that sport is only a means, and that it is merely a matter of knowing how to use that means correctly, and of demanding at least a minimum of spiritual activity along with it. But the necessity of being obliged to make such demands while using such means is precisely what repels us, because we have so little confidence in this approach. It is putting the cart before the horse. We are fooling ourselves when we depend on methods which have nothing to do with Christianity; we are fooling our young people when we let them think they are really Christian, whereas they are not. Something is wrong, because both we and our youth go at this thing for different reasons; we for their spiritual advancement, and they to have a good time. The diversity of purpose gives rise to necessary conflict, or, at the very least, a frittering away of apostolic opportunities.

It is probably necessary to say again that we are not opposed to sports in themselves. This is not the place to go into a discussion of physical culture. The stumbling block here is the lack of religion in 'Christian' athletics, precisely because boys in church teams think that they are performing an act of religion by playing games.

True enough, these teams do provide fine opportunities for individual spiritual instruction. What we are saying is that there is a disproportion between the results and the effort involved in attaining it, especially since that effort could have been used elsewhere. Take the picture as a whole, and you will see that nothing is accomplished for the community. Neither faith nor morals are appreciably bettered; Mass is no better attended; the sense of what it means to be a Catholic is not any keener. Possible anti-clericals or enemies have been changed into indifferentists of a vaguely sympathetic nature. That is not much to boast about. Even the good Christians in these groups are not trained for the apostolate; their spirituality is not enlivened, stirred up, brought into action.

Yet, if they cannot find their amusement under Church auspices, they certainly will go elsewhere for it.

This is a frequent reply, and it is a valid one, up to a point, for many activities besides athletic ones; we have made this argument a yardstick for our use of a social club. Many a priest has come to the point where he wants so badly to have the young around him that he unashamedly lets the club become nothing but a welcome relief to parents who are more than glad to be free of the care of their own children.

We have let our people become so used to this that it is not unusual to hear parents complain when the recreational facilities are not opened immediately upon the completion of the school term. We are really performing an anti-social function. We are encouraging mothers to neglect their children when we are so willing to take them off their hands.

Concerning this, there is an excellent little pamphlet by a Chartreuse Father entitled *A Reculons;* it is old, but still revolutionary. In it the author shows that many of our parish activities aggravate rather than alleviate the evils which they are supposed to combat; they miss the roots of the problem, and they are carried along in the general disorder.

Because we wanted to avoid this pitfall, we refused to open any regular clubs in our parish. It was just as well, for, if we had wanted to look after the children during all of their free time, we could have had a huge task during the irregular school periods of the war. Instead of that, we have the club open at different, stated times, for the different age groups. That leaves a priest time to perform priestly functions, and it makes parents keep an eye on their own children for a change. Some mothers have even had to give up their jobs.

You will say there is a danger of the children growing up in the gutters. We say that such an outcome would be a shame, but let us look at the question before us. Is it our job, as priests, to amuse children and keep adolescents occupied? Our task is one of conversion, preaching, educating, distributing the Sacraments. If the children are in the gutters, so are the adults, and in a more harmful manner. While we are trying to keep the youngsters happy, their father is in a bar-room, their mother in a cinema, and their elder sisters and brothers are God knows where. Certainly it is a shame to see children being neglected, but it is stilll worse to see adults being ruined, families being de-christianized. It is better for us to bring them Christ directly. If we could do everything, then we certainly should not neglect any aspect of bettering their conditions. But, since the task is so complex, we cannot expect or be expected to do it all. A choice must be made, and it seems to us that the best choice is the one which takes us directly to our function as priests.

We have stopped clubs at Colombes, not merely to rid ourselves of the job of taking care of children, but especially for the reasons which we shall develop in the section of this book devoted to educational activities.

Anyhow, even if we did believe that our aim must be the protection of the young, consider what that would mean! We want them to have their recreation under our auspices rather than see them go elsewhere. Let us be logical. If they go to some swimming-pool, does that mean that *we* shall have to install a pool? If they go off for winter sports, does that mean that we must find a Catholic mountain? How can we expect to compete with all the current fads of hostels, swimming teams, camping trips? If we are going to keep up with every new organization and hobby that the modern world can produce, we must expect to be perpetually in action. Every innovation of State or national authorities in the field of recreation will mean more worries for us. It is better to keep in mind the wise statement of men who know how far afield these activities can take us, when they tell us that we cannot hope to compete with any secular force in the field of recreation. It can offer attractions which are completely beyond us.

Are you trying to say that we should abandon our young people to the evil influences around us?

Of course not. It seems to us that, instead of trying to organize and reorganize, it would be more sensible for us to try to Christianize what already exists. Secular organizations are not our business, and neither is their administration. On the other hand, it *is* our business to try to fill individuals and organizations with a Christian spirit. That opens up a tremendous field to us, and it is a field where our temporal resources, or lack of them, will not be a constant problem.

What we really would like to see is organization of the

58

patronage-type done by Catholic lay people themselves. For example, the Catholics of a neighbourhood could band together in order to ensure decent entertainment at the local cinema. Or the mothers could work out a system of taking care of one another's small children on different days. The young men could organize themselves into a Catholic sports group which would be open to non-Catholics. Little by little, as we Catholics begin to realize what our Faith means, things of this sort will spontaneously arise. A priest's task is to encourage them, keep an eye on them, but never to be himself the artificial cause of their existence. Most of all, he should never isolate our Catholic people from the men and women living around them.

We are everlastingly trying to organize life and society as though we were in a majority! The fact is that we are a very small minority. Our attempts to set in motion all sorts of Christian activities are really nothing but superficial efforts. We may as well admit that we are in a pagan world. Did St Paul, for example, try to channel the recreation of his new converts into Christian lines? If we can stimulate men to become solid, ardent Christians, then the social institutions will take care of themselves. As it is now, all our toil is doomed to failure for lack of fighters; paganism creeps in as though by osmosis. But that is another, later problem.

What we have said against the nursery-patronage was meant only for those which are nothing more than nurseries. To be honest about it, that means, or did mean, the great majority of them; it takes no great acumen to see that most of them are doing nothing for the formation of the children. Small wonder that we question what good, if any, they are doing towards the rearing of future apostles, working-class apostles.

Educational Activities

So much for activity that has no other purpose than the direction of leisure time. It certainly seems that the educational type should be different.

The first thing we want to say is that serious and scientific study has done a great deal to improve methods in the course of the last fifty years. We have moved from purely recreational to truly educational activities, thanks to the work of capable men in the field of child education.

Considering what has been done, and realizing the great and tireless zeal of the apostles engaged in this work, we are most anxious for all to understand that our criticism appreciates these things, and that we know and admit that a great deal of good has been accomplished.

But our aim is to see how our parishes can become missionary parishes, and therefore we have to question whether or not these activities have any special apostolic influence on the mass of working people; not whether they are doing a little, but whether or not they are influencing, changing, shaping that mass. Two possible answers can be given us. Some would say that they are forming leaders who will, in their turn, transform the people amidst whom they live. Others would say that they were having a direct influence on the more important element of the working class.

To limit the debate, we shall consider only the activities which deal with children and young people. There are two questions to be answered:

1. Are they giving the workers the leaders they need so badly?
2. Are they reaching into the lives of the workers?

I certainly can see no difficulty in the first question. Our educational system has no other purpose than the training of an élite, which will, in turn, become the leaders of their generation.

I agree with you that that is their purpose, and we sincerely admire the many men and women who are wholeheartedly devoted to this task. They are always on the look-out for new methods, new findings. Hence it is not a matter of their good intentions, but of their results; good intentions are fine, but, as in any other kind of warfare, they are not enough. What we have to say is not intended as an attack on anyone, and we hope that it will not offend or discourage anyone, despite the seeming harshness of some of our statements.

The first question we want to treat is whether or not we are really producing the leaven that S. Paul talks about. After all, we do have to form and insert the leaven which will spread through the whole mass around us; that is our vocation. And, if we are going to give so much of our time and of ourselves to this task, we should be able to procure proportionate results. They will come only when we do mould men and women capable of becoming sowers of the seed, leaders, magnetic Christians. A necessary condition for this result is to see that the leaven is in contact with the group which needs leavening; it must become an integral part of the group it is to influence.

Look around, and see what sort of leaders most men are ready to follow. Admit that they are willing to be led, but admit also that they refuse to be herded. At least that is the case with our French people. They will recognize leaders who rise out of their own midst, but they scorn those imposed on them by an alien authority. That is a fact, whether we like it or not. Look at those who have become, practically speaking, dictators over some of our factory workers, principally because they are 'like' the other workers, and because they know how to dominate without domineering.

With us the opposite is true. Much of our educational programme seems more intent upon giving us commanding officers than it does upon fashioning real leaders. We get our youth so accustomed to precise commands, to military orderliness in thought and action, that the apparent disorder of their own surroundings bewilders them when they return to it. The result often is that 'our' young people are unwelcome, to say the least, among their fellows; they do not know how to adjust themselves to the needs of their apostolate. We have more to say about this in our section on 'culture'; all we want to do now is simply to point out one of the reasons why we are not shaping the kind of leaders that working people will be willing to follow.

Another error, as we see it, is our regular practice of withdrawing potential leaders from the milieu to which they belong, and doing this at the immature age of twelve or so. It takes no great experience with youth to realize that many of our young hopefuls do not or cannot become what we once thought they might. How can we pick out a bright boy of twelve, let us say, and act as if we knew for certain what he would be at the age of twenty or twenty-five? The facts are against such a policy. No, an élite is not to be picked out ahead of time, nor can it be developed in circumstances completely foreign to the group it is supposed to lead. We must look for it in the element that produces it, youth leaders among the youth, worker-leaders among the workers. If we insist on trying to raise them ourselves like hothouse plants, we should not be surprised that they have all the weaknesses of hothouse plants.

That is only a comparison. Are things really as bad as all that?

It is more than a comparison, and things are as bad as all that. Look at the youths and adults we have trained, and see how out of contact with the mass of people they are. Their Christianity alone is not the cause of this separation, but their tastes also, their reactions. We might say that we have brought forth a semi-ecclesiastical caste with leanings like our own; they are somewhat at home in our circles, but really belong to no social class. Every day the truth of Abbé Godin's observation comes home to us. He said that our young people are fairly good, but that they have no influence over their companions.

At the beginning of this book we referred to the question of whether or not Christianity has softened men. The answer is that Christianity, real Christianity, does not and cannot; but our training can and does. We think that we are moulding an élite-corps; we are actually producing docile, conformable men and women.

Look round and see the youth we have formed. They are recognizable in any neighbourhood on any job. Of course this is partly because they are Christian; they cannot behave just like those around them, because they realize that many things are forbidden. Also we see in them a smile, a charitableness, a goodness that results from Christ being in their hearts. All that is good. The sickening part is that they are so often prim and mincing and artificial, like puppets turned out in our shops. They behave in a superior way compared with their poor benighted neighbours and seem to have lost the ability to be natural. That is the result of our training. As if it were not bad enough that this should be the unconscious result, some of us even aim at making Catholic Youth aliens among their own surroundings.

Once, when I was a young priest, I had charge of a girls' group. One of these girls worked with her sister in a factory. The nun who was organizing the girls came to me one day and told me that she was going to start giving this particular girl a course in typing and shorthand, so that she could get a better job, and get away from that terrible factory. And yet, at the factory, she and her sister were the only fervent Catholics, the only witnesses to Christ in that hotbed of modern paganism. The nun had her way. The girl did leave that terrible factory; within a few months she had also left the organization. She had gone up in the world, and her sister, her family, her old friends had become distasteful to her.

Everything about our training seems pointed to a final product which will be polished to a bright middle-class lustre. In the face of this we express surprise when our graduates are unwilling to go back to their native working class. We have made this practically impossible.

I remember a young girl I talked to one day. She came from a very poor family, and her father was a communist; without the girls' group she would have found it very hard indeed to persevere in the Faith, especially now that she was working. I asked her if the work was very hard, and she said that it was; she found the days long, and looked forward with longing to the nights, when she could come to meetings and activities with the Catholic group. I tried to explain that God meant her to work and to influence others at her work by means of the Christianity he had given her; it made only a slight impression. So then I asked her if she had joined the Jocist Movement, because that group was more pointed to the apostolic work she could have a chance to do. Yes, she had joined, but the games and good times of the girls' club meant more to her; that was not so bad, for she was young. But her real reason for clinging to the first group was a dangerous one. She kept away from the Jocists because 'factory-girls' went to that!

Consider how serious are the three self-betrayals contained in this girl's story. She is dissatisfied with her work, with her apostolate, with her own class of people. And this is no exception; it is more typical than anything else. Even though this girl was good and unusually intelligent, this was the result of the training we had given her.

A few years' experience with real apostles among the working-class will clarify the difference between the young people we produce and these militant young workers. Any chaplain of Catholic Action will admit this as an obvious fact, but parish priests do not seem able to see it. The reason must be that the latter are so engrossed in their parish activities that they do not realize how different real life is.

It seems strange that, if our organizations can produce Catholics who go to Mass and support the Church, they cannot also produce militant apostles.

Sometimes they do. Many a boy and girl from out of our midst has become a fine Jocist; better than average in fact, because of the background of good habits gained. But this only happens sometimes; it is not the general thing.

Some priests will tell us that the Jocist girls have been lucky to be able to use already existing parish activities as a recruiting source for themselves. On the contrary, it has spelt ruin for entire Jocist units. It has resulted in a loss of zeal, in an unconcern for the workers they are meant to convert; it has resulted in little groups around the priest, with no thought and no capabilities of influencing the very ones to whom they should bring Christ. Our modern pagans instinctively shy away from this sort of Catholic, and when ex-Jocists of this kind do try to approach the non-Catholic workers, to speak their language, the attempt is artificial, forced. Instead of real, accepted apostles who could transform their whole group, we see Catholic gadabouts, worried about this or that social function. They have become hot-house plants.

It is evident that our young Catholics are not sufficiently concerned with the conquest of their pagan companions; they have no burning zeal to make Christ known to the Gentiles. Why?

That is the difficulty. At the risk of exasperating our

readers, we are going to be honest, and say that we have not the answer. The defects of the parish activities, as we have described them, are an almost inevitable accompaniment of the good features in them. For those who did not see the defects because of the apparent good results, we wanted to clarify the issue; that is something in itself. Beyond that, we can answer the question we raised, only by these two reasons.

One is that our youth becomes accustomed to, familiar with our tremendous religious truths. It is a glorious thing that they have prayed, gone to Communion, and lived Christian lives from childhood; but it is also true that they have become so used to these mysteries that their grandeur, their greatness is dimmed. A new convert will realize better than they what the Christian life and sacraments are, because a bottomless void has been filled in his life, whereas the Catholic youth has never been conscious of this emptiness. We have raised them in an atmosphere where, unlike the world outside them, everyone thinks and reacts as they do. That means that they cannot grasp the urgency of the need of bringing Christ to the world. They are not haunted by the vision of a rejected Christ because they do not realize, concretely, that he is being rejected. They have not had to find the pearl of great price for themselves, and so, they do not feel impelled to call others in to rejoice with them. They cannot quite imagine themselves as apostles.

A good example of this attitude came up at a recent Jocist meeting. Some of the members were converts, and these were discussing, with great animation, the progress of their apostolate in a certain neighbourhood. Another member, from a group which had gone to Catholic schools and societies since childhood, lamenting the fact that her group was so timid, asked the others how they went about this process of explaining Christ to non-Catholics. None of the converts could answer, because none of them had thought of such a problem; it was a matter of spontaneous words, based on the individual situation they were facing. The others felt lost, because they needed plans and procedures; this was one result of the marshalled formation they had been given by us.

The second reason we can bring forward for the lack of apostolicity in our own youth is the excessive concern for their own salvation and perfection which we have drilled into them. We tell them that their own soul is the most important thing in the world, that they must not go with anyone who might endanger their salvation, that there are persons, places and things which they must avoid for their own good. Everything that we tell them seems pointed to that question of personal salvation. Everything is accepted or rejected according to whether it will advance or retard this. On that basis it is hard to see why we should be surprised at their lack of zeal for the conversion of the mass of men. We have given them instead an instinct for spiritual self-preservation. Add to this the tendency already in us to do what is easier, to stay with our own rather than break into a new circle, and you have the development of an 'ordinary' Catholic. We talk about those 'outside the Church' as ones to be pitied, to be prayed for even, but without a serious thought of going out to them and bringing them to Christ.

Being in contact with so many groups, we have noticed a great many things. One of them is the difference between Jocist members and members of parochial societies. The latter, when they are teased or scorned for their 'religion' tend to find solace with others of their own kind. The former, on the contrary, take such reversals undauntedly, and get into lively discussions about how to break down the opposition. One group shrinks; the other thrives on this sort of thing. That does not mean that the youth we have trained are useless, nor that they have no concern at all for the apostolate. That is not so. But the striking thing is that this concern was always an individual phenomenon; it was always a case of working on one prospective convert, one who seemed better than his pagan companions. And the method was almost always the same, namely, getting him to come round to the church for some activity or other. It is very difficult for our youth to see that influencing others does not necessarily and inevitably mean getting them to do something 'religious'.

One way in which we can improve the formation and

education of young Catholics is to associate the older boys and girls with us in the task. This explaining to others will help them learn Christianity better themselves, and they will be more capable of presenting it to non-Christians. However, in this association we must make sure that they avoid a serious pitfall; we must make sure that they do not cease to be militants precisely because they have become 'leaders' of others. Often it happens that working for the betterment of those who are already Catholics softens us when it comes to the battle for the non-Catholics, as we have seen. If we withdraw a really zealous apostle, so that he or she can be a stiffening influence on younger Catholics, we run the risk of letting that apostle become content to work among his own, and to neglect the ones who need his fervour even more. In a parish which has comparatively few apostles from the working-class, and which has a great proportion of pagans, it would be a serious mistake to withdraw such firebrands to any great extent. I have seen such mistakes made. One case comes to mind, that of an eighteen-year-old factory worker who had been given charge of a group of boys of twelve to fourteen. When the curate suggested to him that he would be able to do better work in the Jocist movement, he said that he preferred to stay where he was. An apostle was being wasted, at least to some extent.

Choosing these helpers in the work of training the boys and girls is no easy matter. We have to decide whether they are going to be taken from student groups or from among the workers. If we pick students, it is almost impossible for them to prepare the youngsters to live as they must live, in surroundings which the 'better-class' teachers do not know. And if we pick workers, we are retiring choice campaigners from the field in which they can do most good; besides, as we saw above, it often means that such workers lose contact with the ever-changing problems of their own milieu. The dilemma is still with us, but at least we can see some of the difficulties in our way.

Too often we priests fall a prey to the temptation to use those who come forward to help us in a way very distantly related to the direct apostolate. We press them into service as typists, messengers, stage-hands. That may be good for the parish budget, but it is hard on zeal. Worse than that, it can compromise, in the eyes of their fellows, the very persons who could reach the non-believers; if they come to be considered as the 'priest's right hand man', their influence is definitely impaired.

One other important danger that most of us have not avoided is being honest enough to realize that the programmes we launch 'grow old'. We have all seen this happen. A new curate comes in, starts a movement that goes along for years and does splendidly; but the young people who were foundation members lose their youth. Still, we hate to replace them with new leaders, because those are so sincere and so devoted. Before we know it, the organization is stagnated and the youngsters consider it as something for the 'old folks'. What began so well has outlived its usefulness, even though it continues to exist.

That failing is an inescapable factor in every living thing.

It certainly is a natural failing. A solution is not easy to find, and we certainly do not recommend the suppression of all activities just for this reason. What we must do is to recognize the limits of our organizations, especially as regards the conquest of the non-Christian world around us. We cannot go on telling ourselves that we are forming the élite of the future, and be satisfied with that. Seeing the danger will help us avoid it. It takes courage to keep on measuring and calculating the exact worth of our programmes; it takes more courage to keep on making the necessary adjustments.

Still, even if our parish activities are not giving us the leaders which we should have, they do at least console us when we see the great numbers engaged in them. And, sooner or later, if the children continue to come to us, we shall have conquered the pagan world. Even if we do not succeed in transforming it here and now, we certainly shall.

We have heard all this before. It is true that our work has had good results and that children have grown up and founded Christian homes precisely because of our parish activities. That helps a great deal. We said at the beginning of this chapter that the network of parochial work of this sort has done much to strengthen and invigorate the Church in France. Without meaning to disparage past praise, we still are compelled to say that there is another side to the picture.

For years, for generations, we have been told that our control over the children of to-day means the support of the adults of tomorrow. For years we have heard newly-arrived priests say that they were here to make a fresh start in the parish. Somehow it seems contradictory that, after fifty years of 'controlling' the children, we still have to dream about the support of the adults, and every new priest has to go on making fresh starts. Something is wrong.

A young Socialist told me, a long time ago, that he supposed we were satisfied to have so many children around us. But he went on to tell me frankly that that was no proof of any great strength, because he planned to send his children to the parish club until they were about fourteen; then he would take them back and make good Socialists of them. The years in between the Church could have; it was easier for him and his wife that way.

We must find the reason for these spasmodic, perpetually spasmodic, efforts. Some of the fault lies in the fact that we lean too heavily on parish activities, and especially on those dealing with children, in our attempts to advance the kingdom of God. We work with children too much, and not enough with families. A child is yet to be formed; he is plastic. More often than not it is his anti-Christian family which has the preponderant influence upon him. In a later chapter the question of the apostolate to the family will be treated at length; all we want to do here is to show the connection with our work among the young.

Part of the fault is found in the fact that our clubs have to have rules and regulations and supervision. The children are kept well in hand. Obviously not all of these rules have anything to do with Christianity, but a confusion does arise in the minds of the children. Consequently a great many never really enter into the spirit of what we are trying to do; their lives and the intended formation of our guidance remain in two distinct spheres.

Surely there are enough varieties of organization to contact and influence every type of person.

That is questionable. However, the primary aim of any organization of ours should be to instill Christianity; whether that is done by camping, by study clubs or by any other sort of group is secondary. One important point to remember, lest we tend to develop blind faith in groups and clubs, is that many Catholics do not care to join any of them. This type of person, too, merits attention, and the fact that they seem not to co-operate should not be misconstrued. It does not necessarily mean that they are less Catholic than those who come to parish functions. When I came to this parish, my predecessor handed me a list of names of persons who, he said, were 'not active'. As a matter of fact, a good many of them were exemplary Catholics, and they did respond, when given a chance to be apostles. They had not joined the ordinary type of parish activity simply because their family life and religious security had made joining unnecessary.

The conclusion is this. We must not delude ourselves into thinking that parish societies are everything, and that anyone not interested in taking part in them is nothing. We can, if we do not check ourselves, reach the stage wherein we think of non-co-operators as selfish, apathetic Catholics, and treat them as such. In reality they often are very much the opposite.

Looking at this situation from another angle, is it not an inspiring sight to see young priests so zealously engaged in the care of all the associations usually present in our parishes? It must be a providential outlet for their fervour.

It is inspiring, and we would be the last to dampen their zeal, or to say, from our ivory tower, that they are not accomplishing any real good. That would be most displeasing, to say the least, to many an old priest who has given his whole priestly life to just such work. No, it would be wrong to deny that they are doing good, and that the work is doing them good. In connection with this, we would like to make one issue clear. When we say now, and again later, that we favour the suppression of these parish activities, we do not mean that we advocate this course because such a suppression is easier for us priests. Young curates who are quick to take our advice often support us simply because it will mean less work for them, or so they think. They are wrong on both counts.

In the apostolate, it is most unwise to destroy what we cannot replace. Hence, if we have no substitute, we should keep things as they are until we get one. When we talk about doing away with children's groups, the reason is so that we may devote our time and abilities to the adults. That general norm must be believed in and followed.

Once that is understood, we should like to go a step further, and expose a very real danger. When young priests come into a parish, they are usually given charge of the youngsters; very seldom are they given any other type of association. It seems to be generally agreed that the purpose in life of young priests is the formation and guidance of everyone in the parish under eighteen years of age. What does that mean? Simply that we are channelling the most powerful stream of priestly enthusiasm into the solitary outlet of the youth apostolate. Besides depriving the adults of at least some of this benefit, we also are encouraging these new Levites to fall into the old misconception about the children of to-day equalling the adults of tomorrow. And the adults continue to be neglected. If a young curate is assigned to take charge of children's groups, as well as being asked to preach, hear Confessions, visit the sick, etc., he can hardly be blamed for having no time left over for the grown-ups.

The fact that the clubs and leagues take up so much time is not as serious as is the fact that they also consume our interests, our dreams. We become almost incapable of seeing any other means of advancing the reign of Christ; we become almost unconcerned about the progress of the parish as a whole, provided our club or our group is doing well. Even seminarians are infected by this outlook. They all seem to have ideas about what they plan to do for the boys and girls, once they are ordained; very few have done any intensive thinking about the parents of those children.

Surely there must be a way of reaching both young and old. This is a hard thing to say, but it almost seems that we priests are consoling ourselves at the loss of the men and women by turning to the boys and the girls. When the men lost interest in religion, we concentrated on women;

when adolescents began to abandon us, we made intense efforts to keep the little ones around us. They are easier to handle, more receptive. Woe to us, though, if we narrow the limits of the kingdom of God to the point that it includes only the little ones!

You mentioned, a while ago, the danger of being too ready to suppress all parochial activities. Is the opposite danger, namely, to be too engrossed in them, equally wrong?

We think it is. It leads us, among other things, to the smug attitude of mistaking the following out of a programme for a really worthwhile result. Péguy mentioned this when he wrote about the tendency to be satisfied with what has been done rather than with doing things. He meant that we call a group together, draw up a constitution, make a programme, and then sit back. True, we keep trying to make the meetings interesting, but we look upon the task as more or less completed. We are, unconsciously, in the process of losing the realization that there are others to be gained for Christ, outside this tiny circle. We can honestly tell ourselves that all our strength and ingenuity is being expended, and that we are not 'taking life easy'. The first statement may be true enough, and the second too; but we are not doing enough once we let this one field satisfy and absorb us. We are coddling ourselves. Rather than seeking out the others, the ones who will not come in, we have established our sway over relatively easy subjects. Most of us will deny the truth of that conclusion; in fact, most of us do not realize that we are doing just that, because we are in good faith. The fact still remains.

There are, of course, many priests who have established a balance in their work; they do reach both young and old. Many more have been rendered practically useless for the adult apostolate by their excessive preoccupation with the children. It is much easier to talk to a group of impressionable youngsters than it is to preach Christ before those who might ridicule us. Gradually, imperceptibly, we grow soft, and the easier ministry becomes our total ministry.

Another evil feature of our times is the fact that priests, though few in number, are compelled to do so many things which are not properly or necessarily priestly.

We agree with you. A modern priest, more than ever before, should be free to exercise his priesthood to the utmost, and not be bound down to merely temporal and material tasks. The activities that we have been talking about do much to bind him down, because a priest engaged in them has a thousand worries about how and where to find the resources to keep them going, and about drawing up their programmes or organizing their celebrations. Go into the room of the average curate, and see the proof of this for yourself. You will see a room cluttered with bazaar posters, lists of names, programme notes, publicity placards, and a host of other similar things. It is a pity that successive generations of priests have been and are being forced to limit the possibilities of their priesthood in this fashion.

What is your conclusion from all that you have said about educational activities?

Adhering to the principles we stated when we began this book, we will draw no conclusion. Everyone who reads this work has problems which are locally, psychologically, and spiritually, different from those we find at Colombes. Hence, every reader must make his own conclusion, based on his own situation. All that we can say is that, while these activities do seem to be a necessary part of the modern apostolate, they were not always so. The time seems to be approaching when they will no longer be so. Good judgment and true zeal will indicate when and how changes can be made in each corner of the Lord's vineyard, and also how these changes can be improved upon as the times continue to evolve around us.

Would it be a correct conclusion to say that you are against the types of activity about which we have been talking, and that you favour their suppression?

Not at all. We should, we admit, be deeply interested in the work of a priest who found the courage to replace all these groups with a programme of intense direct apostolate. It does seem to us that such boldness would be rewarded with more success than meets our present efforts, but we have not the courage to take such a stand ourselves; nor could we, therefore, advise it to anyone else.

Looking over the history of the Church in the last fifty

years, and it was during this time that the system of parochial activities grew up, two facts stand out. One inspires us with confidence; the other is disturbing. The first shows a gradual growth from the material to the spiritual. For example, the club used to mean little more than a nursery; nowadays, it is becoming concerned with the formation of the young. Another example is the evident growth from groups interested only in providing athletic facilities for boys and girls to our present concept of study clubs. All of that is good. The other, the disturbing factor, is the tendency which all these groups seem to have, namely to settle into a routine. Zeal, especially for those outside one's particular circle, is all too easily lost.

One certain fact is the need for a change, for a renewal of spirit. The ardour and magnanimity and apostolicity which inspired the beginnings of all these activities must be rekindled. It is not enough to be concerned only with the smooth running of what someone else started; it is definitely not enough to be enmeshed in details and administration, and thereby to lose sight of the purpose of these details and this administering. All that we do for God must be touched by the eternal youth which the Holy Ghost will give the Church.

CHARITABLE ACTIVITIES

What do you have to say about the works of charity?

Here we have a really integral part of the Church. Like Christ before us, we must be concerned with the misery of mankind, and find in it a means of bringing men to know and to love and to serve him. Ever since the time of the Apostles, the Church has been helping the poor and caring for the sick; until the Revolution in France the Church bore almost the whole burden of these works of charity. Since the Revolution the State has taken them under its wing, but the Church must continue doing what she has always done. It is a logical consequence of the command to love our neighbours, body and soul. Unlike the State, we act from a motive of supernatural charity; the government can give money or clothes or food, even as we do, but only the Church of Christ can give his love.

Over and above this general picture, there are certain peculiarities to be remembered in the exercise of charity in a working-class parish, when that charity is meant to have a missionary purpose. One is that this need not be intended as propaganda; despite the apparent contradiction here, the statement is absolutely true. The very fact that we love our neighbours will be a more powerful witness to Christ than any attempts we might make to capitalize on it will be. If our motive for practising charity is to draw others into the Church, the recipients will shy away; they will realize that there are invisible strings on our gifts. If, on the other hand, our motive is the love of God, that love will shine through the gift and through the giver up to the very source of the love; we need not worry about that. When we help anyone and then try to get that person to come to Mass or to approach the Sacraments, he cannot help but recognize our mixed motives; and, usually, he refuses to be bought by our aid.

In a parish which is predominantly pagan, the distinction between 'saviours of souls' and 'builders of Christianity' must be kept in mind. We want the non-Christians around us to be forced to see and acknowledge the love which animates the Church of Christ. Those whom we serve must be able to see Christ in us before we can expect them to draw near to him. The sight of Sisters of Charity at work can do more for propaganda than any clumsy exhortations we might try to foist on the poor or the sick.

In connection with this, we would like to say that charitable organizations are best conducted by nuns and lay people rather than by priests. The basis for that opinion is found in the Acts of the Apostles, for they ordained deacons to do that sort of work and to leave themselves unencumbered in the preaching of the Gospel. If the clergy take up the direction and administration of charity, they are using time which could be better spent on more direct apostolic endeavours, and they are jeopardizing the results of the charity. Everyone knows that priests are Christians; there is no need of labouring that point. Moreover, they will give the whole programme a clerical aspect, which is, as we know, most undesirable. For the good of the mission

·cause we should prefer to see priests staying out of this field.

One more thing. The very generosity we show to the needy may, and often does, lead people to believe that we are wealthy. Anyone who knows the limits of our wealth and the hard task we face in raising it, will smile at such a thought; but, for the mass of men, that belief is more evident than the Gospel we preach. They see 'the Church' giving away money and food, and they come to the conclusion that, somewhere and somehow, she has an inexhaustible supply of money. So they are willing enough to help relieve us of some of our excess wealth, and the good which our generosity intended to do is destroyed. The answer to this difficulty lies, we think, in placing the control of charity directly in the hands of those most interested in it, namely, laymen of the same social and economic standing as the majority of the parish. The Jocists or the family groups which exist in most parishes would be ideal directors. They are among the people and of the people; they know better than we who really needs help, and what form it should take. Moreover, they will not be suspected of 'clericalism'. Hence they make the best witnesses of Christ in the dispensing of his Charity.

PROPAGANDA

You mentioned propaganda activities a long while ago, but you have said nothing about them.

No, because we wanted to keep them for a special section. They, above all others, are specifically missionary, and we include under this heading any and every movement which has as its sole purpose the spreading of Christian truth. The only exception we make is the spoken word, because we want to leave that to the section devoted to the question of preaching. Here we mean the written word, the stage and the cinema.

Are they such an important part of the Mission movement?

Indeed they are. An especially noteworthy fact about them is that most parishes use them. Like everything else, they are delicate instruments, and we must make sure that they are not so mismanaged as to hurt the cause.

The press, first of all, is of primary importance. By the press we mean anything printed, ranging from pamphlets to newspapers. The printer's ink will reach out to those who will not come to hear our words; it provokes thought where our personality or presentation might be an obstacle; it answers questions which men would not have the courage or the inclination to put to us. Consequently, a 'pagan' parish which neglects this avenue is losing golden opportunities. There need be no fear of using it too much; notice how secular and other far-seeing groups make use of it! By it we can reach those whom we want to attract, and whom we cannot hope to convert by speech.

Now for the precautions we must take. Knowing how our people love to classify everything, we must be wary in our recommendations of any particular paper. The one we do recommend or permit to be sold in the church becomes, in the minds of the parishioners, 'the' paper of the Church. We can protest as much as we like that people should realize that we are not giving complete approval to anything and everything that newspaper may say. The fact remains that the ordinary person does not and will not make such distinctions. We cannot go to the absurd opposite and refuse to praise any newspaper, because the good ones do deserve our support; discretion and investigation of the ones we approve is the answer. One of the chief reasons for the gulf between the Church and the people is the widespread opinion that the Church has become the property of the 'upper' classes. Consequently it is not difficult to see the harm we can cause, if we act as agents for a publication which gives support to that false conviction by its attitude.

The wealth of truly Catholic newspapers makes our support of the smug, intransigent ones all the more senseless. There are so many which deserve all the backing we can give them that it pains us to see a parish priest praising them as 'anti-communist', 'anti-Protestant' papers. Of course, even the best of them does not speak officially for the Church, but they are doing a tremendous work in bringing Christ back to the souls who have seen him only in caricature. We must do what we can to gain support for them, but, in so doing, we must not endanger the good they are doing. By that is meant that no one should be able to see in our recommendation a basis for calling these newspapers 'clerical'. Let them do their own advertising.

What do you think of the value of a parish magazine?

It is a powerful weapon in the missionary conquest we are striving to accomplish. In it the priests of the parish can air their opinions freely; by it the news of the whole parish is circulated. The magazine can continue where our Sunday sermon left off. All of these things it can do and more, if we really use it as a mission weapon. That means sending a copy to every family, and not just to those who pay for it; the ones who pay for it are already convinced, and have less need of the Physician. The ones who are convinced can be persuaded to help by paying for the copies sent to the others. Another cardinal principle is that we direct its articles, its tone, its approach to the non-believers, because its prime purpose is a missionary one. While it is good for parishioners to see their name in print and to read about the different social functions of the parish, such a carefree attitude is out of place in our circumstances—at least, as a main purpose. Nor should it be 'pious,' because sugary spiritual items will repel the audience for whom these bulletins are intended. Its style, too, should be watched, so that the articles will be direct, unaffected, friendly in tone. A good thing to remember is that people who read relatively little read very carefully; students or educated men fall into the habit of swift reading, and the retention of only the main points. But the average working-man is a thorough reader, and he attaches more importance than we ordinarily would to the written word. Hence the care that we take to present truth in a telling way may be rewarded by the return to Christ of our readers.

Many parishes use a syndicated magazine which is made up elsewhere, and intended to be general enough to interest the average parishioner anywhere. That may be cheaper in money, but it is more costly in souls for anyone who plans to use the publication as a propaganda agent.

The format and colouring and the use of cartoons, etc., are important, but we have found that they are not worth too much trouble; the contents are more vital than the dressing. Our audience seems to have a higher regard for the pure newspaper type, rather than for the illustrated papers. As long as we keep forever before our minds that this publication is intended for the non-churchgoers, we shall avoid making it a social paper, a humorous magazine, or a purely 'parish' bulletin.

You also seem to be avid users of pamphlets and notices of all sorts.

Indeed we are. It seems, sometimes, that we consume almost as much paper as the 'Propagandastaffel' did in its heyday. We are staunch believers in the power of the printed page when it can be easily read, and when its few main points are high-lighted.

We have formulated two classifications for these placards and pamphlets; one is used to attract people, and the other to provoke thought. For us, the first type is more sensible, because our purpose here is to let everyone know that the parish exists, and that it exists for everybody. When we can give the impression that these notices are practically personal letters (and that often happens!), so much the better. As long as we refrain from putting out too many, too often, they retain public interest. Another practical point is in their distribution. Instead of mailing them or slipping them under doors, we have found that the best method is to have a militant put them in the hands of the recipients. The personal touch is heightened, greetings are exchanged, and an invaluable contact has been gained.

Naturally, tracts which are being used to spread ideas and cause comment can be distributed much more often than can the invitation type. They can be made into a graphic apologetic vehicle, not with a 'defence complex', but in a positive, confident way. Different seasons of the Church year, like Easter and Christmas and Pentecost, are natural occasions; incidents or problems of the neighbourhood also can be utilized by an intelligent editor.

Even billboards, of a striking nature, can be pressed into service. We have several regular spots scattered around the parish, with placards that tell the time and nature of services at the church; besides these, we put up special ones for extraordinary events, like a mission, a feast day, etc. At least they show the vitality of the parish, and publicity of this sort is especially needed to-day, when we tend to relegate religion to a forgotten corner of our individual worlds.

What do you think of parish cinema shows?

Frankly, not very much. As films are now, a parish priest is out of place when he acts as a distributor for them; unless he means to present only religious pictures, he is, to say the least, wasting his time. Our fond hope is that soon Catholics can have some good historical films produced on subjects like the beginnings of Christianity, Joan of Arc, and the like. To try to use the ones circulating now is an impossible task for a priest. We could go into more detailed reasoning, but it hardly seems necessary. Any energy that we want to spend on films would be better directed to getting the lay people to make sure that the cinemas in their neighbourhood are not showing objectionable films.

And the production of parish plays—what do you think of them?

These are not, of course, as dangerous as films, but they are not much more useful as missionary tools. The time consumed by them is hardly proportionate to the results. Most of us have been subjected to enough parish plays to agree that they are pretty tiresome, and that they involve so much delicacy in assigning rôles that they often end in animosities, not Christian charity. Sometimes, of course, a really good production is staged, but this is more the exception than the rule. No, a priest with a missionary goal cannot afford to waste the time and talents which these plays consume.

SPECIALIZED MOVEMENTS

Is your approval of the specialised movements as qualified as was that of the other types of activities?

On the contrary; we have nothing but praise and support for them. These organizations, like the Jocists or the family groups, have a completely praiseworthy purpose and result; they are meant to instill Christianity into particular groups and places, and they are doing that splendidly. They represent the apostolate of 'like to like', as the Popes have asked; they are made up of fervent apostles in action at the factories, offices, and in the neighbourhood.

By this truly Catholic action the transformation of entire classes has been begun. Religion has come out from the sanctuary in a very real effort to sanctify the world. Jocist and similar groups realize that men will not answer appeals to come to Mass, but that they will listen when Christ is brought to bear on their social, industrial and individual lives. Rather than stress the happiness of heaven, a solidly Christian attempt is made to better present circumstances. Scoffers and doubters are shown that the Gospel is not ethereal, but real and practical; apologies are replaced by proofs of an ideal way of life. The very men and women now engaged on this work are proofs of what can be done and of what is being done, because most of them are drawn from former scoffers and doubters and bewildered souls. We cannot say enough to show how highly we regard this manifestation of the apostolate—especially in a working-class parish like ours.

And yet the general impression seems to be that movements like these are engaged in by 'Revolutionaries'. They are respected, but treated with a certain reserve, as though they had a different purpose than the parish.

What you say is, unfortunately, too often true. Basically, such an attitude is founded on the idea that a parish means only those who come to church; we discussed that at length a while back. If anyone does hold to that idea, he will logically see the Jocists, etc., as 'non-parochial'. A priest who wants to hold processions and services for his 'regular' parishioners will not be over pleased when the Jocists do not show up at them; they may be off for a day of recollection, or engaged in an apostolic effort—but they should be at the church or in the procession—or so the priest thinks. Recriminations and questionings follow, and ill-will is established. Our Catholic lay apostles are human too, and very often discouragement and bewilderment result from this attitude of the priest.

Are the results of this type of apostolate as impressive as is sometimes claimed?

There is no denying that they are impressive. And yet, after approximately fifteen years of toil, the Christian Workers' Movement is still in a spasmodic state, with the expected results still distant. Before criticizing the apostles engaged in this work, we should look nearer home for the blame. We priests have supported them but poorly, and have preferred to keep around us and around our more petty concerns the young people who could have become valuable recruits to the cause. We have been negligent in making ourselves efficient and useful directors of consciences for the Catholics who especially need us. Anyone who has talked to these militants knows how poorly we have fed them with the spiritual substance we are supposed to dispense; they want to taste the things of God more than we make it possible for them—or so it seems. How then can we point an accusing or a self-justifying finger at them, when we have made ourselves obstacles to their fervour? The time we could give to forming and directing these hungry souls we prefer to spend in other ways.

Even when there are efforts to form and guide these apostles, the misconceptions of a priest can be almost as harmful as positive neglect. It is a serious business to undertake, this guidance of modern apostles. Any priest who does enter into it must grasp that he is to help them see Christ in all the affairs of modern life; he is to fan an already brilliant flame. For that undertaking the priest cannot be mediocre himself. He cannot fall back upon shopworn clichés; he cannot preach at these men and women who ask to be guided. They have questions to ask, problems to clarify, and listening to a one-sided sermon will not aid them. A priest who sees in their inquiries only impudence is woefully wrong. A priest who would like to see these young Jocists more orderly, more systematic, more demure, has missed the eagerness for Christ that is driving them on.

Another mistake is the opinion that a combined 'study and formation circle' is the ideal way to guide groups like the Jocists. In them Christian doctrine can be discussed and applied. While the idea has its good points, it has defects also. The meetings, once or twice a month, are too far apart for a sustained and profitable study. The ready-made explanations of our teachings are too abstract and too general to help its members apply them to existing conditions. Last but not least, such study clubs often wean the apostles away from the real problems that surround them to theoretical study of principles. Connected with these defects, it is not unusual for a priest to ask that a Jocist unit become more 'integrated' with the parish. Since he means by that that the unit is to devote itself to strictly parish activities, the net result is the collapse of another Jocist cell. Tangled in a maze of parish functions, the unit loses both its appeal and its internal fire; those 'outside' are gradually forgotten.

We must keep our hands off movements like these, and permit them to remain what they are intended to be—lay-movements; true, the priest must guide them in doctrine and in spirituality, but, instead of trying to make them clerical, he must leave them free to exploit their peculiar appeal to the non-believing world. Let us never give place to the absurd idea that laymen and laywomen are no more than our messengers, sent by us to persons and places we cannot reach ourselves. They are infinitely more than that. As members of the Mystical Body, they, too, have their mission to accomplish; they, too, have a duty to preach Christ when and as they can. Paternalism or kindly tolera-tion from us will stamp out the spark of apostolicity that God has given them. All of this we have done, but we must change.

So far, you have spoken as though the clergy were entirely to blame for defects in the specialized apostolate. Are there no faults on the other side?

Of course there are. Not infrequently laymen fall into a certain snobbishness, a feeling of self-sufficiency; they neither need nor want any interference from the priest, and they let that be known. The final result is, of course, a lessening of the good that each could do by co-operation, and a loss of the supernatural character of the priesthood. Lay Catholics must realize—as indeed almost all do—that the priest holds a sacred trust from God, and that he is essential to their sanctification. Without that source of holiness they are incapable of bringing Christ to others, and their very purpose is defeated.

Another weakness is the ever present danger of becoming so involved in the struggle to better working conditions and family life that the original purpose of making Christians of these pagans is forgotten. We are not saying that the Jocists or similar movements should not try to improve these human factors, because that is an important means of bringing men to Christ; but we are saying that Christian apostles should not degenerate into mere humanitarians. Our starting point and our goal must be supernatural, or we shall never make Christians of them. Better, happier human beings, maybe; but not Christians.

There is another, more subtle, defect to which these particular organizations fall heir. In their zeal to convert the great numbers outside the Church, they falsely think that they must attract great numbers. That will come, but not immediately. Sometimes, when the meetings or entertainments they sponsor are crowded, it looks as if their work were succeeding wonderfully—and therein is the worst part of their error. Numbers have dazzled them. Instead of realizing that many who came, came to pass the time, and many will not come again, our Catholics see success in the offing. In such a concept the fundamental principle of contact with Christianity has been swept away. If Catholic Action is to be 'successful', it will be a matter of influencing individual souls, of drawing them to the stage where Christ will become visible, desirable, attainable. The fact that a meeting is 'mammoth' is not, in itself, a good thing. A few pages back, when we discussed educational activities, we tried to bring out the point that such activities were not defeated completely by the presence of mediocre Catholics; because the very nature of the work protects its participants from serious contamination by alien influences, even the lukewarm Catholics were more or less safe. However, in work such as the Jocists do there is no such protection. Two harmful results will follow from this mass contact. One is that the Jocists themselves will be affected by the pagan majority to which they have come. Secondly, if mediocre Christians only are put in contact with non-Christians, there is certainly little hope that enough of the spirit and love of Christ will be given off to draw those who know him not. In either case the results are lamentable.

It does not follow from this that we, as priest-guides, must forbid all large-scale contacts, nor that we leave the task of meeting pagans only to the real apostles. The first is not necessary; the second would spell the death of the zeal of many an embryo-apostle. What we must do is to indicate the possible dangers underlying this type of action.

The last weakness we shall mention is also a widespread one; it consists of the transition into administrators of those who began as magnetic Christians. Routine, excessive paperwork, ritualism—these are shoals to be given a wide sweep. Only by work in the market places, only by a quenchless thirst for souls will the working apostle find his place in the Mystical Body.

Going a step further, do you think that such activities as these have a place in parish life?

Positively. In any parish they are a priceless testimony to the place of Christ in everyday life; they are living teachers of what it means to be a Christian. As such, they are infinitely more important than the parishioners who come for Vespers, but do not manifest God to their neighbours. We priests must grasp this, must see the peculiar value of their work, and must not try to measure it according to the usual parochial standards. We have grown used to placid, docile followers; we must become used to this new species. If they seem rough and hasty, part of the appearance is due to our own excessive gentility. Instead of being horrified at their outspokeness, we might well learn to speak more of their language. Instead of letting our dignity be offended when they plan a celebration without consulting us, we might well take fire from the sparks of their impetuous zeal. Instead of threatening to disband these anarchic Christians, we might learn to rid ourselves of the moss of routine grown up around us.

Someone told us about a pastor who became infuriated at the Jocists in his parish because they were so casual towards his position. He mounted the pulpit of the church, clad in surplice and stole, and delivered a terrible denunciation of the group. Waving his stole, he cried, 'Here I am in command, and you must obey me; this is the symbol of my divine power'. Since no one knew the symbolism of the stole, his climax drew more titters than feelings of awe.

It will be easier for us and for these lay-people if we realize that they are tremendously conscious of the necessity of making Christ known; they cannot rest under the weight of that consciousness. That explains much of the apparent carelessness we see in them, and it is a motive we disregard only at the risk of displeasing our common Lord.

Consequently, we ought to direct their efforts into the mission-effort of the entire parish. Some parishioners will object to working with them, either from haughtiness or from fright; we priests must show these Pharisees that no one can be a Christian who refuses to be an apostle. Anyone who feels superior to these young workers, because of being better educated than they, or because of belonging to some one of the 'better' parish societies, is not worthy of them. Such a one needs instruction, and needs it badly.

The actual direction of their efforts can take different forms. Here at Colombes one of the priests is the director of the Jocists; he enables each of the different committees within it to keep in touch with the priests who have charge of separate sections of the parish. In this way, the whole set-up is co-ordinated and informed on the needs of the whole parish. The ideal would be to have a complete Jocist movement in each of the portions of the parish, but the present plan is the nearest we can approach to this ideal. A better picture of how these lay-apostles actually work will be given in our treatment of the 'direct apostolate'. All that we say here is that there is a very definite and very valuable use for these movements in any parish.

How do you attain unity among such diverse activities, so that each of them is truly parochial?

That demands care. Obviously, not all are suited to the same kind of work, nor could all of them work alongside one another. We have to find a place for each. One way to attain this unity—or rather, to prevent disunity—is to make sure that the really diverse ones have their own places to meet; if the Jocists had to assemble at the parish hall, the reaction might not be so good. To avoid clashes of background, it is a good idea to have something like a club-house or meeting room for the Jocists away from the parish hall. Besides the other reasons given, it enables them to do more good, since they are not 'around the church'. Hence, in realistic ways, we try to find the place for each movement, where each can do the most good for the whole parish-mission.

THE DIRECT APOSTOLATE

All that you have said sounds impressive, but it also sounds rather strong. Even though the activities you have criticized do have many defects, they are, at least, functioning and doing some good. What would you substitute for them?

Please understand us. We are not negative critics, and we are not so much interested in the exactness of our criticism as we are in the hope that some good may come of it. We priests are few in number, and the work at hand is overwhelming; the days when we could worry only about our own churchgoers is past. Somebody has to call for a change in attitude and approach, and we have tried to do that. Like every other priest we have made many a mistake since the day we came from the seminary, and we are still making them. We are not setting ourselves up as examples, but we have come to the conclusion that a direct apostolate is more efficient and more valuable than the indirect activities we were analysing. What we have said was not meant to tear down other men's work, but to help to clear away misconceptions, and to show why we came to the conclusion that there must be a better way to bring Christ to this world of ours.

Tell us how you reached that conclusion.

It was a gradual process, made up of the mistakes we made and the thinking we did. At the risk of boring you, we will try to give a short description of the road we travelled.

As far back as we can remember, the effect of militant Catholics upon unbelievers astounded us. We used to be afraid that their new-found zeal was too direct, too brusque, that they would repel the pagans they contacted. Instead of that, we saw that they were respected even by those whom they could not convince. After noticing that fact for years, our slow mind finally saw the light. This was one of the answers! By contacts here, we mean personal ones, and not mass meetings; although it is easy to draw crowds, it is difficult to reach the souls of individuals in them. Incidentally—speaking of mass-meetings—there does seem to be some value in those such as the Salvation Army holds. Over and over again we have heard it said by people watching them that at least the Salvation Army had the courage to profess what it believed. Maybe we could use something similar to good advantage.

Apart from that our observations were of personal conversations, of words said with confident conviction to a neighbour or a fellow-worker. The resulting conversions are amazing. Consequently it seems only reasonable that this man-to-man way ought to be considered; it does produce results, and it certainly goes directly to its goal.

Nearly all of us will admit that the modern adult needs to be given a reason for living. His confusion is crying for an answer, and that answer must be true and inspiring and spiritual. It used to be said that we only had to let them recall the religion of their youth and they would come back to its practice when this confusion came upon them. Not so now, because this generation knows nothing about religion; we cannot remind them of mysteries they never knew. And yet they need something, disillusioned as they are by the hollow claims of progress. They know they need something, and they will grasp at spiritual values, materialists though they still are. They are weary of *ersatz*, distrustful of glowing promises, and more or less convinced that happiness is not here. Religion, because it will be a new experience for most of them, has a splendid opportunity at this very time. What Christ is offering will be revolutionary to these jaded revolutionists, and their souls will open up to his warmth.

It sounds as though you would like to herd them into our ranks.

Not quite. The day when priests could herd souls is gone, and we are not lamenting its passing; as a matter of fact, because that day has gone, we need the direct apostolate all the more. If we tried the old system of starting a 'movement' to rechristianize them, they would stay away in droves; they have had enough of 'clubs' and all the rules and regulations which accompany them. Here in France we saw that reaction after the Liberation. In their minds there already exists the idea that the Church is nothing but another 'movement', another organization that wants a lot of members, and wants them for its own selfish reasons. There is no point in approaching them in such a way that their false opinion will be strengthened.

Our goal now should be to show them a spiritual, disinterested Christianity that is 'lived', not 'joined'. We must show them Christ, in all his love, all his grandeur, all his beauty, so that they will come to him, and make him the source and the end of their daily lives. That is our goal.

How shall we do this?

Not by activities, but by our words, our deep convictions, our unglossed presentation of his gospel. One of the most telling ways of doing all this is to have one soul in contact with one other soul; to have the believer tell the non-believer exactly what happened to him. The doubts and fears that were washed away, the experience of what it is to know Christ told by an intense believer—this is what will win our modern pagan proletariat. We priests cannot achieve this by our old willingness to 'enroll'; it is not a matter of getting members, but of transforming the unbelievably dreary spiritual lives of these people. We cannot do it merely by opposing error and false doctrine, but we must show them the way, give light to their paths and something positive to their lives.

Nor shall we do it by our text-book apologetic arguments. Some, of course, will be interested and even convinced by them, but the mass of men are not swayed by our well-reasoned arguments; they heard so many errors so well expounded during the war that they believe it possible to prove anything. So, when we try to prove the truth of Christianity from historical or social or philosophical premises, they are unmoved.

Well . . .?

We shall do it only by showing them what Christianity is and what it demands. That sounds over-simple, but we believe it to be *the* answer. It is what our militants do; they never hesitate to state what this religious transformation entails. They explain the personal nature of this call of Christ and the necessity of a personal reply. Unlike most modern priests, they are not slow to speak about the last ends of man, not of the fire and brimstone, but of the fact that an end does exist and that it must be considered. They make the after-life sound like a personal problem of the one they are trying to win, and, more often than not, it actually is. Personal, individual adherence to the Christian way of life is what militants work for, because it is the only real conversion. Despite what we said about the necessity of working on the mass of men, and on social or economic groups as a whole, it still remains true that we must win each member of those groups as individuals. We are so convinced of this that we consider it the very essence of our priestly work.

So, it seems, did St Paul and the other apostles. We like to go back to those cornerstones of the Church and find in them the answer to our present problems. Somebody wrote somewhere that Paul, if he were to come back to our world, would become a newspaperman. Maybe so . . . However, there is no conjecture about the fact that he did convert his prison guards, that he did talk religion to people he met in the public squares, that he did gather acquaintances and strangers together to talk to them about Christ. We know that he did win people to Christ, and in these ways. Why not, we ask ourselves, use these same methods to-day?

People will not be surprised if we bring up the subject of religion; they accept that as our 'job'. Hence, it seems foolish to take roundabout ways for something they expect us to do. Since priests are so few, it is foolish to burden them with complicated and indirect approaches to possible converts (as we said so often in our section on activities), when a simple, direct avenue is open to us. We simply cannot do everything, and if, as we have found, the direct apostolate brings us more souls than we can satisfy and guide—then it certainly is impossible for us to give time to anything less immediately apostolic.

Another reason why we are boosting the direct apostolate is the fruit of much reflection. We have seen priests who 'succeed' in the ministry, because they are good choir-masters, or athletes, or theatrical producers. Without sarcasm, we came to the conclusion that such men could not

90

have been given Holy Orders simply because of the possession of these natural gifts; while it is helpful to have them, they certainly have no necessary connection with the priesthood. They certainly are not intended by God as the basis of a fruitful ministry; nor does he condemn all those not possessing any such natural endowment to mediocrity in his service. It seems to us that Christ, who calls and picks his priests, must send them to a work which will be possible for them simply because they are priests. To say that he measures the worth of his anointed servants by any other standard than the love that impels them is more than absurd. And so, from that conclusion, we say that the direct apostolate is the one form of his service in which his love suffices, no matter how ungainly a priest may otherwise be. He loves the souls which God made and redeemed, and he wants them all to come in; they, in turn, respond to this single-minded, selfless motive, and they will come in. At least, they will come in more often than they do through our present oblique efforts.

These arguments sound fine, but we still want to know how you go about applying this direct apostolate.

First of all, we shall try to explain the priests' part in it, because they are the foundation of the whole structure. Later on, we will tell you how the parishioners are mobilized and what weapons they use.

In the course of a priest's day he makes a great many contacts with souls. Here at Colombes, all the priests consciously try to use these meetings, these incidents, as stepping-stones towards winning a soul for Christ. For that, the human side of the priest is very important. Lest we seem to be contradicting what was just said about the sufficiency of the priesthood itself, we hasten to explain that we never said that human qualities had no importance; we were talking about the false opinion which makes these accidentals more important than the priesthood itself. With that understood, we can proceed. Because we are men, we must use our humanity to draw our fellow-men, just as Christ took on our nature in order to make it possible for us to come to God. Hence the priestly character within us must manifest itself in human understanding; Christ must be

91

visible in our poor flesh. We have to use little things, like smiles and handshakes and friendliness, just as he would have done in our times. We priests will admit all this, and we have heard it repeated in one way or another since our seminary days. It might help us to see whether or not we are living this truism.

Allow me to project myself into all this, to bring out what I mean by using little things. I have a wretched memory and cannot remember whether I met this man or where I met that woman. It has been terribly embarrassing many, many times. To avoid such embarrassment I have got into the habit of greeting everyone by a wave or a nod or a smile. At first the people were astonished to have the parish priest greet them on the street or in stores, but, after a while, they got used to it, and even liked it. Now they greet me and the other priests first; everybody does it. In fact, a priest friend of mine says that he can tell when he is in Sacré Coeur parish by the fact that everyone starts saying 'hello' to him. Maybe a story like this seems to over-simplify the apostolate, but it has been my honest experience that the step from a greeting to a conversion is not very long.

There is no appeal here for priests to become back-slappers and hail-fellows-well-met. All we advocate is a natural, casual way of talking, an ability to make small-talk. 'Weeping with those who weep and rejoicing with those who are joyful.' We want everyone in the parish to feel that we are with them, that we are theirs. That is not easy, as indeed we know. We have a different background, a different vocabulary, different tastes. I remember a young priest who tried to strike up a conversation with a mill-worker. In an effort to break the ice between him and the old man, he mentioned that his father had been a mill-worker too. 'Is that so, Father? I never would have thought so.' What was intended as a polite compliment contained a lot of bitter truth. We tend to become artificial when dealing with men and women who work for a living, and they, in turn, are uncomfortable in their dealings with us. Whether we actually are or not, we act and sound like people from the 'other side of the tracks', and that handicaps our efforts in the direct apostolate. To overcome such drawbacks we have to make intense efforts to know our people, their jobs, their troubles; a good beginning for us is to stop them in the street and chat a bit, or to stop at a doorstep and exchange a few words with a family. There is no great value in accepting dinner invitations, and there can be great harm in them if we go too often to one house, or if we go only to the more comfortable ones.

Chatting in the streets or doorways sounds like very inadequate contacts.

There are better ones; for example, the ones with people who drop into the sacristy for one reason or another. That drab little sacristy can be a haven of peace for many people who come in for some 'business' purpose but find there a priest who is interested in their life and troubles. Too often those who do come—to arrange for a baptism or wedding—feel awkward and bothersome; they are not asked to sit down, nor is there any evident pleasure in the priest's face or manner. The sacristy has the atmosphere of a city hall office, and the priest acts like a hurried and tired clerk. How foolish we are to miss these opportunities! Here we have a chance to talk with parishioners we rarely see. We have a chance to show that the marriage or baptism they came to arrange is no mere ceremony, but an integral, essential part of their lives; we can make Christianity, immortality, grace come down from the realm of the abstract so that these intangibles will fit into these lives. These sacristy visits are precious opportunities . . . But we are in a hurry to get back to the priests' house and read the paper; so, according to our temperament, we growl or joke our way through the interview, and the opportunity is lost.

It would be foolish, of course, to believe all the reasons that people give for their abandonment of religion, but so many of them say that it was due to some sort of upset with a gruff priest that we should be most careful not to give anyone a chance to blame us for his loss of God. It is a question of fact, not of logic. We know priests that we are afraid to approach, and we can imagine what his parishioners go through. We know Catholics who have gone through a civil marriage rather than go back to a parish

93

priest who ranted and raved when they went to him during their engagement. These are small things? We are not so sure.

Other good contacts can be made at the time of the children's First Communion. We always meet the youngster's parents, and always manage to get across the idea that it would be a wonderful sight to see the father and mother receiving our Lord on that morning too. Many a parent had not even thought of that; when reminded, many do receive. Again, when somebody stops us to bless a medal or a rosary, it never hurts to stop and talk a while with them. I recall one young girl who asked me to bless something one afternoon, and simply because the priest stopped and talked with her, a tragedy was averted in her life. Or again, in the confessional we can do incalculable good for the cause of Christ. It honestly seems to us that a priest could make an apostolate of staying around the church, and talking with as many people as he could, those who come in for a visit, to pray at a statue or to light a candle. Even though he could not and should not start a conversation with everyone, his time and effort would be rewarded in the tears he dried, the worries he calmed, the doubts he answered.

All of these examples are commonplace, and purposely so. They prove that even 'routine' ministry is filled with opportunities for the direct apostolate—if we want to look for them. A priest who is awake can find many such provided he is willing to 'waste' time with people who are half-way willing to talk to him. He can be a brusque official, or he can be a priest.

One thing to remember is that all our other efforts will fail unless we are kind and sympathetic. We may have grandiose and clever ideas about liturgical revivals, about sermons, about all sorts of activities—but they are as sounding brass and tinkling cymbal. Unless we are loved by the ones we are trying to win, and unless we love them, we shall most certainly fail. The greatest of these is charity still.

I suppose that you encourage people to drop into the Priest's house when they want to talk over something?

Yes, we do; and since we do, we try to make sure that

nothing in our house is going to make visitors feel uncomfortable. We are in a working-class parish, and so we try to have our furnishings and their arrangement simple and ordinary; if they are luxurious, none of our people will feel at home. If they do not feel at home, they will not come back, and we shall not be able to influence them as we might have done. Abbé Godin advised priests to make their rooms fit the type of person they were trying to attract. For example, young students would feel at ease in a somewhat disorderly, cluttered room. In any case, our quarters should never be sumptuous and ornate, for our lives should be a reflection of Christ's and not a denial of it.

You seem to be restating Maritain's slogan about 'being one with your people'.

Exactly, for it is our purpose in life to become Christ to this portion of his inheritance. We are not meant to be kings, but commoners; we are to be neighbourly, friendly, sympathetic, kind, so that it becomes almost second nature to us to 'feel' with our people. During the war we did our best to be like this to everyone around us, and it was noticed and remarked upon by many a person who never came inside the church door; we had a chance to bring Christ to souls who once would have scoffed at the idea that they would talk to a priest.

Besides all these more or less accidental contacts, tell us about the ones you deliberately make.

As we shall explain, we make systematic visits to every home in the parish. For a parish priest, no other function of his ministry is so pressing, no other function is so suited to reaching the great numbers who are his parishioners despite the fact that they do not come to church. The Curé of Ars believed this, and practised it. The immense size of city parishes makes it much more difficult than it is in country towns, but organized teamwork by pastor and curates can accomplish it. We cannot expect to find everyone at home, but we always come back, like insurance men. All this takes up a great deal of our time, but it is time well spent—better spent than it would be on something less directly connected with the preaching of the Word of God.

Lest we be misunderstood, let us make clear here that the

purpose of our home visits is not simply to pass the time of day, not simply to hear the family gossip; we come to talk religion, and that is what we do. As a matter of fact, we firmly believe that we are expected to talk about God and his affairs, and that we scandalize people when we carry on a completely secular conversation with them.

How do you go about these home visits?

There are several possible ways. One is to go from house to house and from street to street until the whole parish has been covered. This method (if such it is) takes too long, and produces little fruit; we might start a few children coming to catechism, and we might get a nodding acquaintance with a great many people. Never much more than that.

Another way is to use the information that our militants can give us about different families in their neighbourhood, and to use the publicity that they can give others about us. It helps, when we come into a house and know a little about the family; we can understand better the reception they give us, and we can stress what we know will interest them most. More about all this later.

Still another method was suggested by a priest in Nice, namely, the idea of home-meetings. Basically, it is the same practice as that used by the apostles, for they used to gather the faithful in someone's private home, and there preach to them. We arrange with a militant Catholic to come to his house on such and such a date; he and his wife tell the neighbours, and invite them over. Of course, many refuse, but enough always appear to make the meeting lively. On the appointed night, one of the priests drops in and gets the conversation round to the subject of religion, gradually or abruptly. Since everyone present has come for that very purpose, it is not a hard subject to approach. Once the awkwardness and novelty have worn off, the questions come thick and fast and the evening is all too short. The priest leaves fairly early, but the hosts can easily prolong the discussion after his departure; it is an excellent occasion for them to do their own type of apostolic work and to wield an influence over their own kind.

The above description is not meant as a typical one, because these home-meetings have almost infinite possibilities; we can get neighbours together, or parents, friends, members of the same nationality or workers from the same factory. They are not hard to organize, because our militant Catholics are proud to work on them, and people seem to want them; their timidity vanishes in the sincerity of the questions they want to ask. Because of the great interest in some particular matters, it may be advisable to start a home study-club, so as to treat the subject more satisfactorily, especially since we can be quite sure that the interested parties are not likely to come round to the church for their answers.

Even your routine ministry must furnish occasions for 'follow-ups' at homes.

It does indeed. When somebody comes to the rectory to arrange for a funeral, we always drop in at the house to express our sympathy. Before or after baptisms, we have a talk with the parents of the child. At marriages the priest who has charge of that section of the parish visits the couple. Before All Souls' Day the families of those who have died during the past year receive a personal invitation from us, asking them to come and pray for their dead. Every feast day of the Church provides similar opportunities.

What kind of a reception do you receive?

Generally, people are surprised to see us, but most of them are friendly enough; there are plenty of exceptions to this, but they are, after all, exceptions. What does not surprise them is that we bring up the subject of religion; they really expect that of us, even the non-churchgoers. Our own timidity is more of a barrier than any hostility from the people, because, strangely enough, we priests do feel awkward when we talk about Christ to individuals— especially to men. It does take courage, and a little persistency, too, because men usually tell us that they will call in their wife—as though religion was her concern. So we have to bring them around to see that religion is not a strictly feminine preserve; usually it is not too difficult, once we gather the courage and the skill for the correct approach.

Yours must be a satisfying and absorbing priestly life.

Honestly, it is, precisely because it is priestly work. It starts from God and ends in him. Remember, too, that it is

97

the work of a 'team' of priests, who pray and work as a closely knit spiritual unit. Because of the size of our heavily populated parish, we have split it up into sections, each one in charge of one member of the team—but not mathematically nor exclusively. By that we mean that the division is not made by dividing the number of priests into the total population, nor by making each priest 'king' of his own territory only, with no concern for the rest of the parish. Rather, each is given a 'district' as his special field, but with the understanding that his section is an essential part of the whole parish, and must be so considered.

Do you think it would be a good idea to make parishes smaller?

Yes, we do. It is a physical impossibility to know our people in these over-size parishes; consequently, Christianity no longer reaches the 'excess' population. In the Middle Ages, when our cities were much smaller, and our Christianity much more real, there were many more places of worship. Nowadays we have one church for from 25,000 to 100,000 parishioners—and we wonder why the worship of God is not a reality for all these souls. How can it be? When Cardinal Verdier started building city-chapels, he acted on the theory that the more places of worship we have, the more Christians we shall have; the results have proved him right, and his plans merit expansion. These chapels should be parishes, and not mere absorbers of the overflow from the main church, because we are firmly convinced that worship must be a community function. Connected with the number of parishes is the number of priests assigned to them. As things are now, assignments are made on a basis of how many practising Catholics there are; one parish will have ten priests, while another will have four— even though the total population of both is about the same. Naturally, there are more confessions, Masses, etc., needed in one than in the other, but we are thinking of missionary work. Surely that cannot be considered less important than the 'routine' demands on priests.

In any case, it is usually possible to use curates more efficiently. Instead of giving them some particular activity for their personal charge, as we sketched further back, we think that it is more practical to give each of them a part of the parish as his mission-field. When every curate is concerned only about his own little groups, how can he be expected to see the parish as a whole? How can he be expected to reach those who are not a part of his group, or of any group? When, on the other hand, activities are cut to a minimum, and each priest is a part of a team that concentrates on the entire parish, it is possible for him to be a real priest, a real missioner. Over and above the practicality of such a plan, it has the tremendous advantage of making a new curate feel that he is wanted and needed, and not merely 'assigned'. He can develop his talents and his gifts to the utmost, in union with the rest of the curates and the parish priest. He has a chance to know his section and his people intimately, and he can develop and direct militant Catholics on the spot. He can live his apostolate.

In a set-up like this the pastor has a delicate rôle to play. He must know how to direct without domineering; he must encourage initiative without creating jealousy; he must realize that a young priest can see and accomplish possibilities that are beyond his own powers.

However, despite all the good that this decentralizing process can do for priests, this is not its sole purpose. It also stimulates the life of the parish as a whole. As Cardinal Suhard said when he came to the diocese, 'The whole parish must become a mission field, and it can be this by becoming a community'.

Explain how you go about convincing your 'regular' parishioners of the missionary purpose of the parish.

First of all, we have to drive home the idea that a Christian has to be an apostle! Never delude yourself into thinking that this is an easy matter. If you try to preach this to the stolid, respectable, 'Sunday-Mass' Catholics, you will know what we mean. It takes time and repetition, by sermons, conversations, pamphlets, until the churchgoers begin to see what we mean. It takes time and repetition. An example of what we mean can be seen in two very different reactions to what happened at a Midnight Mass here a few Christmasses ago. One man—a pillar of the church, by the way—complained because he and his family were unable to get good seats. The church had been packed by persons not seen at Mass from one end of the year to the other, and he thought that preference should be given to the regular churchgoers. Another parishioner happened to speak to me about the crowded condition of the church, but this one was glad about it. She admitted that she had not been able to see the altar, but seeing strangers in there meant more to her than her own satisfaction.

I mentioned these two opposite reactions to the congregation in the following Sunday sermon, in order to help impress them with the fact that we are more concerned about 'outsiders' than about our faithful flock. Gradually they come to understand; gradually the vision of the thousands around them who know not Christ becomes a reality to them too. We stress the importance of the Pope's statement that all Catholics must take part in Catholic Action, so as to help them see that their apostolate is an essential part of their Christianity, and not 'something extra'. Once that concept is grasped, the Christian community unconsciously becomes more of a community; its concern for those outside the Faith draws all its members together in love and in labour.

The second stage, following upon their conviction of the necessity of becoming apostles, consists in making apostles out of them. Many of them will confuse Catholic Action with the apostolate, as indeed do many priests. Many of them will think that they are meant to round up children for catechism class, to talk couples into having their marriages 'fixed up', or to persuade those that have lapsed to start coming to Mass or Novenas. All this is good, but it is not what we mean or what we need. We are not trying to patch up the ills of the world around us; we are trying to rebuild it completely. For that we need real militants who will fill their surroundings with the spirit of Christ, so that men and women will want to know and follow this Christ. We are not interested in gaining recruits for our church services, but we are passionately interested in gaining recruits for Christ. The creation of this new and revolutionary Christian atmosphere depends on the common efforts of each and every Christian; it cannot be left to the members of the specialized movements we mentioned a while ago.

Every man has his own little world to influence, to change, to christianize. That is what we must do as united individuals.

Convincing people of this necessity is difficult, because most of us would rather be apostolic in some easier way; we would rather face the shamed embarrassment of lukewarm Catholics than the possible scorn of non-believers. To put across the proper persuasion we use every possible means— talks, meetings, personal conversations; in the district meetings, the priest in charge constantly emphasizes the influence we should have on some particular point. Maybe this particular street has such a bad reputation that we must have a militant family living in it; maybe the corner barber-shop needs instruction on the kind of magazines it provides for the customers; maybe the daily line-up of people waiting for rationed food is a good place to discuss Christianity.

Every Sunday we announce the special meetings to be held in the different sections of the parish, and we try to make every single Catholic feel invited to them. We want every man and woman to take part in them, and we also want to prevent the growth of the idea that only certain persons are charged with the carrying out of the Christian revolution. We cannot afford to permit the 'let-George-do-it' attitude take root. Some, of course, are actually unable to do much active work, and these we try to impress with the necessity of earnest prayer for the programme. Apart from these few exceptions, every single member of the parish has a rôle to play, according to the talents and the circumstances that God has given him. There is a diversity of gifts, just as there was in the early Church; we do not expect the same results from varying abilities. All that we are trying to convince them of is that each of us has a definite and responsible work to do for Christ; no one is excepted.

Any attempts to organize this apostolate are dangerous. Personal zeal is what we are after. Once a priest erects an organization, with officers and meetings and by-laws, zeal will suffer; that is a proven fact. By some strange quirk in our minds we seem to believe that the founding of an association is equivalent to the success of that organization, and we stop trying to do what we joined together to do. No, we need a group of apostles who will be in a constant state

101

of change, because their work demands constant change; we want apostles who will see the work as never done, because what we are trying to do is, actually, never completed. Consequently we avoid regimentation, lest zeal die. The place of a priest is to guide, to point out possibilities, to talk over results; he is not supposed to rule and dictate, by means of an organization that he, and not the Holy Ghost, brought into being.

Will there not be confusion and overlapping between what the parochial and the specialized militants do?

There will be overlapping, but that does not necessarily imply confusion. The Jocists, and the like, can reach and affect where parochial apostles cannot. After a little experience, each group finds its proper field.

Once you have convinced and trained your parochial apostles, what concrete missionary work do they accomplish?

We have to provide the tools and the occasions, because most of them need more than their original first fervour. They can use the parish magazine that we mentioned previously as a source of ideas to talk about; that is one reason why we insisted above on the magazine's being a propaganda weapon, and not a mere social sheet. They can bring up for discussion some one of the adapted feasts to be held in the parish church; when prudent, they can even invite some interested non-believer to attend, knowing that he will be able to understand it. Every detail of our parish life, because it is directed to the winning of the 'outsiders', is built on and for the apostolate, and a convinced believer can be shown how to use it as propaganda.

What part do you assign the family in your apostolate?

It has a primary place; we hope to bring that out as we proceed. It is our firm conviction that past efforts in the apostolate have been disappointing precisely because they neglected the family as an object and a means of conquest. Somebody would do well to make a study of this; here and now we can say only a few words. It seems to us that we should be preparing our young folk for Christian marriage, and helping young married couples to make their homes Christian. These new families are our real source of strength for the immediate future, and we should exert our influence on them. Catechisms, for example, should be so written as to have some value for parents, as well as children; to do that we can expand and supplement the ones now in use. Our ceremonies, too, should leave the family together. There is no point in separating a family as soon as it comes in the door of the church, sending the children to one part of the church, the father and mother to others. Our entertainments should not split up a family either, but could easily be directed to the entire group. One of the most valuable aspects of the direct apostolate, with its home meetings, is that it definitely tends to bring families, as such, closer together; it unites them in a common cause, in direct reaction to almost everything else around us.

Do your lay apostles really have the time and the ability to carry out all these ideas?

That is a difficult question to answer. Instead, we should like to put forward an idea of which we are fond, one that we have thought about for a long while. Why should we not have a Congregation of Sisters who would devote themselves solely to the direct apostolate? As things are now, we have flourishing Orders doing almost every conceivable kind of work, ranging from orphanages to hospitals. Not for one moment would we even hint that this work is not valuable; it is indeed, and we would be lost without it. But, if there were a Congregation which would devote itself exclusively to a door-to-door preaching of Christ, without any secondary motive, we believe that a tremendous uprising of Christianity would result. Everyone accepts nuns and respects them. In lay or religious dress, they could be the Christian equivalent of social workers, or the Western equivalent of mission catechists; better still, they could provide the Catholic equivalent of the evangelical zeal of the Salvation Army.

It is time you gave us a concrete example of your experiences in the direct apostolate.

All right, but remember, we are not setting ourselves up as models. What we say will show our failures as well as our success; being ordinary, and not learned men, we have learned as we went along. For whatever it is worth, we will give you a summary of the past five years' work in the direct apostolate.

We began by a month of intensive preaching on the

apostolate itself, and kept referring to it all during the year. At the end of the month we called a meeting for all the faithful of the parish, and explained our ideas on decentralization. To make the notion understandable, we split the meeting up into groups based on our division of the parish into districts; the priest in charge of each told them that they were each to sit in a special part of the church at next Sunday's Mass. The majority expressed doubts that enough people would come to fill each section, but, thanks to advertising, the doubts were not realized. Merely dividing up the seating arrangement in the church is no great feat. The important fact is that it made the people conscious of their own districts, and convinced them of the *possibility* of influencing it. That was the beginning. That year was spent in trying to find out how to go about holding meetings and making visits. One of the curates tried the door-to-door system, but it was impossible; another hit upon the one we now use, namely, letting the militants in the neighbourhood direct us. We tried mass-meetings in the different sections, but they involved more entertainment than apostolicity, and we abandoned them.

The second year we spent in organizing—dull perhaps, but very necessary. By the third year we were ready for home-meetings. At first, we simply mentioned the idea, and waited for reactions from the people; there was no point in forcing our plans on them. It took two months before anyone invited us to hold a meeting in his house, but, from then on, they spread rapidly and are commonplace now. As a matter of fact, the lay-people did far more than we to make them succeed; they know each other so much better than we can hope to that they adapt the discussion to the audience with remarkable skill. During Lent of that year we held thirty-four such sessions; of the average ten or twenty persons present, normally only three or four were practising Catholics. We started with themes like the Church's attitude to Nazism or the problem of deporting workers into Germany; gradually we shifted to the reason for wars, the problem of suffering, the Providence of God. The questions we were asked gave us clues as to what to talk about, and they also revealed the torment in the souls of the questioners.

By the end of that third year we got the idea of district missions, and began to plan for them; during the fourth year we started to hold them for two weeks in each section of the parish. The first week was spent with all of the priests trudging from street to street and door to door in that particular section, as directed by the curate in charge there. We went into every home and we talked religion, frankly and proudly and lovingly—and usually we were more than welcome. Some came back to Christ on the spot. In our talks with them we emphasized that this mission was for their neighbourhood, and that we thought they would like to take part in it; the personal appeal and the localized setting made a good impression. At night we held home-meetings all over the chosen area, and they were very well attended. For the last part of the second week we held services at Church; a sermon reviewed the general principles we had been stressing, and then we acted out the Passion. After each tableau, during which a priest chanted the Gospel story in the vernacular, the preacher outlined the main points of the scene; we ended with an appeal for a return to God who made and saved us. The audience was impressed, we know. They were not immediately, nor always, converted, but, for many of them, it was the first time they had heard the word of God. That was something. We had taken down the names and addresses of all present, and we followed up this contact.

Unfortunately we could not keep up the pace we set for ourselves, and now we hold one or two such missions a year. Together with these, we have what we call the 'Journey of the Blessed Mother', just as many another parish has had before us. On Sunday night we bless one statue of our Lady for each of the parish sections, and give it to a militant from each one of them; he is to see that the statue goes from home to home, staying one day with each family. Most families wanted to keep it longer. As a matter of fact, it has stayed as long as two weeks in places where we had thought no one would welcome it! Along with the statue goes a little leaflet of prayers to be said before it by the family every night. This 'Journey' has some marvellous advantages. It gives us an occasion for visiting every family which keeps it; we bring

105

a little memento of the incident, and we talk about what it means. Also it enables the militant in charge to gather all the families together on the last night of the devotion; the priest comes over, too, and explains our Lady's place in our lives. Only two or three houses closed their doors to the Blessed Mother, and many who took her in were complete strangers at church. She is loved, and she will help those who do not realize that they need her help.

All that we described here is but a fragment of the sum total of possibilities in the direct apostolate. Whoever tries it will find new and different approaches, based on local circumstances. The field is inexhaustible.

I do not want to quibble, but there seems to be some inconsistency in the fact that you used Lent as a special time for these missions. Lent has no meaning for non-believers.

We agree with you, but, remember, these were not ordinary Lenten Devotions; they were an offensive during Lent. We chose that time because the Church means those forty days as a special time of grace; all the mortifications and prayers of Christians are calling down God's help in a special way during this season. Moreover, it is a time intended for effort and for reflection on what it means to be a follower of Christ. That is why we chose this season. If we had done no more than gather together those who already believe, your protest would be valid; but, since we made every effort to draw those who do not believe, and tried to make the service appeal to them, we have to justify our choice of time.

What results can you show?

For one thing, there has been a steady increase in Easter Communions. One Easter Week we were approached by six adults who wanted to receive Baptism or First Communion; what they said to us shows that it is the cumulative effect of our work that counts and not the individual conversations or meetings or services. One of these men told us that we had visited him several months ago, but that he had received us coolly, because he was not then interested in religion. Later on, he heard us speaking at a funeral, and he realized for the first time that we evidently believed what we preached! Still later, he accepted an invitation to a home-meeting, and was forced to think seriously of the message of Christ. He came to Mass for Palm Sunday and Easter; the sight of everyone going up to receive Almighty God made him realize that he was an outsider, and he determined to ask for Baptism.

The story is an unadorned fact. It is a proof of the gradual penetration of a soul by repeated and varied approaches to Christ. It is a testimony to the worth of the direct apostolate.

Still, everything that you have been doing is for adults. Are you completely neglecting the children in these plans?

We were wondering how long it would take you to get to that. It is usually one of the first objections put to us by fellow-priests. There seems to be some necessary connection between priestly labours and the care of the children. Despite the impression which our section on clubs may have given, we hasten to assure you that we are looking out for the children too. It is possible to be concerned about both young and old without neglecting either. You see, we are more interested in evangelizing the youth than in educating them; we are not meant to relieve parents of their responsibilities, and we do not intend to do so. We try to give them a meaning of Christianity which will be suited to their age and will also be real and personal. After First Communion, we group them according to districts, and put them in charge of one of their own members, under the eye of a militant lay-person from that section of the parish; their work is that of the junior members of the Jocists.

By a development of their own life with Christ these young people can make him known to their own age group in a peculiarly effective way. They become little Christian communities in their own right, and they bring the influence of their convictions to everyone whom they know. Naturally, they have games and programmes for themselves, under the direction of lay-men and lay-women. Most of all, they are made to feel the meaning of communal parish life, its unity and community. We do not expect these children to be present in herded groups at every church service; we want them to be apostles, and not mere attendants. During the year there are special feasts for them, and they come willingly and eagerly. They are young and are still to be formed. We are content with forming them.

IV DYNAMIC CHRISTIANITY

What do you think of the idea that we must have a Christianity which startles people; a Christianity which is dynamic?

The idea appeals to us very much, even though these phrases are rather objectionable. This idea is founded on the undeniable truth that Christianity is static. It no longer causes any surprise or scandal or admiration or imitation; it has become classified, labelled and forgotten, just as any dull subject is dismissed. When it is discussed, the comment is about its ceremonies or diplomacy, and not about its meaning. It has become part of the order of things, exactly as teachers and judges and doctors have, and it has ceased to conflict with the lives of the mass of men. Christianity is here, but we can forget about it.

Why should this be so? Partly because our Christianity appears to the outside world only as a *ritualistic* system which does little or nothing to change the men and women who practise those rites; partly because we have ceased to be an influential community; partly because Christianity has reduced itself to attendance at Sunday Mass, without any evidence of the vital nature of Christ's teachings. The modern pagans who notice us do not see in us the striking characteristics which caught and held the pagans of ancient Rome. They see only that we are not very different from themselves, and unfortunately, they are correct. We go to Mass, and they do not; that is the extent of the difference for most of us. Christianity has ceased to be 'dangerous'; it involves no risks, no sacrifice, and it causes hardly a flurry in the affairs of the world.

Consequently, it is understandable why non-Catholics should not be interested in investigating the mystery of our Faith, for they see no evidence of it. Nor is it strange that they should be untouched by the burning love of Christ, since his professed followers fail to transmit the effects of his love. We are not obviously anxious to communicate his love, but rather appear to be satisfied with the untruth that each man's religion is his own affair. We are content to leave the rest of the world in its unrealized misery, nor would we dream of startling them by the Cross of Christ which we bear about in our bodies.

Who is to blame for this?

Partly the people, because they should know better and should do better. The greater fault is ours, we priests, because we have substituted ritualism for the Pentecostal flames. We do not demand enough of our people. That statement does not mean that we are too easy with individual weaknesses. We should be 'too easy' with particular failings, just as Christ was before us. We mean rather that priests do not ask enough of the Christian community. Instead of transforming our parishioners into a living, united group, we feel that it is enough to get them to come to services. The more we have, the better we are satisfied, as if it were enough to have the name of Christian and nothing more. We administer the Sacraments, but make no effort to instill into our parishioners a sacramental life. Like the thousands of sects, we want to increase the number of our adherents, while seeming to ignore that we must make God live in man. Even Catholics have lost the meaning of our rites and our outlook, and so people think of them as some sort of 'hocus-pocus'.

What is the reason?

It is obvious. Think of how easy it is to become a Christian. We put a little water on a child's head, and the parents go home to celebrate their offspring's redemption with a pagan feast. Later on, the lad will come for a few years of catechism, ending in a touching ceremony, a sermon that makes all the mothers weep, and the inspiring sight of boys and girls going up to the altar rail for First Communion, the 'church' part of the day is followed by a celebration long to be remembered. Still later, this typical Christian comes to arrange for marriage, and to pay the priest. After this ceremony a new Catholic family begins its existence, without a single distinguishing feature to set it off from the neo-pagan families around it. When the time comes to die, a Christian burial is a matter of course; with it ends the life-span of a 'follower of Christ'.

There we see an ordinary example of Christianity—the religion which once turned the whole world upside down.

When we hear radio orators declaiming about our 'struggle for Christianity', we cannot help but wonder what that phrase means to our Catholics.

How would you suggest establishing these dynamic communities?

Before we offer our suggestions, for whatever they may be worth, there are a few qualifications to be made. When we put down our thoughts on this subject, it is done because we feel that we are obliged to share our conclusions with the findings and hopes of many other priests and lay-people. However, when we put them down, it is with the understanding that the Church is the final judge of what is to be done or not done.

The first reform should begin in our conduct of parish life. The manner in which we conduct the routine affairs of the parish should reflect a burning thirst for souls outside the family of Christ. It should be so evident and so sincere that our parishioners will come to share it. Particularly, we should administer the Sacraments in such a way that the sacramental life we talk about will be understood and realized. In Baptism, for example, we must make sure that the meaning and consequences of this fundamental Sacrament are understood.

Parents bring in their children for Baptism much as they would for vaccination; it makes no difference that they themselves do not practise Catholicism, nor that they have no intention of rearing this child in the Faith. Baptism is simply one of those things that everyone goes through. It is an important social function. You know how it takes place. Most of the men present have anticipated the celebration; everyone crowds around to watch the curious ceremonies, and the god-parents know that they are in for a teasing if they get through the *Credo* and *Pater* without a halt. Worse still is the common practice in maternity hospitals around Paris. The priest walks into the ward and announces that he will baptize all the babies whose mothers are willing. Nothing is known about the mother, less about the father— and yet we pour the saving waters on one and all who ask for them.

It makes our blood boil to see abuses like these and to be the agents of such a farce, and yet the people would think we had lost our minds or our religion were we to rebuke them for their ignorance. What are we to do? It is a terribly hard thing to refuse Baptism to a helpless child. And yet the teaching of the Church, as expressed in Canon Law and elsewhere, is that children of infidels should not be baptised except in danger of death, unless a Christian rearing is reasonably guaranteed. The qualifications required of god-parents is another proof of the attitude of the Church. Moreover, when we baptize so freely, we rob the Sacrament of part of its meaning; it is intended as a sign that this person is now a member of the Christian community, with all the accompanying obligations and privileges. Remember that our Lord said 'No one, unless he *believe* and be baptized, will be saved', and he gave us no permission to forget the first part of that statement. Yet the children we baptize will find it hard to believe and to practise that belief, in the face of daily, practical disbelief on the part of their parents. We are bringing in to the Church of Christ souls over whom the Church will have no influence.

Consider the common practice of missionaries concerning Baptism. They are severe on this point. They have to be. Because they are, the meaning of Baptism is caught and the new Christians are fervent; their Faith means a great deal to them and has a great influence on their pagan neighbours. The same practice, and the same result, was true of the early Church.

Still, refusal of Baptism would drive a family outside the Church forever. There would be absolutely no hope of priestly or lay apostolic influence on them.

That objection bothers us too. However, we cannot permit a very real abuse just to avoid displeasing people. If refusal did become a general practice, the growing generations would have a chance to see Christianity as it is, instead of accepting it as an uninteresting, uncomprehended part of their lives. This is a delicate problem, and we do not pretend to have answered it, even though we did bring it up here. A thing like this cannot be solved by any individual priest, and it will not be solved by anger and tongue-lashings. The old adage about honey rather than vinegar is still true. At every Baptism we must try to explain the importance of

111

this step. All of our efforts come back, as we said so often before, to the education and winning of the adults, the parents. Until the parents have come to understand Christianity, we are at an impasse.

Despite your gloomy picture, it is true that most of these children are sent to you for Catechism and First Communion instructions.

They are, but what does that prove? About eighty per cent. of the children we baptized come back to us for religious instruction, but that fact is little comfort to us. If the preparation were not demanded, the youngsters would not be sent for it; the parents would be satisfied with the celebration only. To show what we mean, there is a classic case in our parish files. There was a lad who had told his mother, over a period of two whole years, that he was a member of the catechism class here; as a matter of fact, we had not even seen the boy once. By chance his mother discovered the fact of his deceit on the very afternoon of the Confirmation ceremony—after two years of unbroken absence! Fortunately all turned out well, and that boy is now one of our leading apostles. However, the incident does prove that parents, even friendly and practising parents, have almost no concern about the religious training of their children. They send them off to catechism, just as they were once sent off, and that is the end of their problem. The motive is not so much to ensure that their sons and daughters will know and love Christ as to keep up an old family tradition.

When one or another of the parents is positively hostile to the Church, the situation is worse, as anyone familiar with the appalling leakage after First Communion will agree. Sometimes the religious training we give to these children of anti-religious homes serves as an oasis of Faith; sometimes the youngsters do persevere beautifully. Yet we have to admit that something is wrong. The Church has had charge of almost all the children of France for the last hundred years—and yet most of those children have left her fold. We might honestly call First Communion day the day of Solemn Apostasy and be done with it. Without exaggerating, we can say that eighty per cent. of these new communicants will have ceased receiving the Sacraments within three or four years. Yes, we have the children—just as we have had every year for the last century; every year we have the same hopes, and every year the same disappointment.

Maybe the blame rests on the catechists?

It is easy enough to shift the blame around, but it is hardly fair to the catechists. If they are at fault, so are we pastors; if we want to cast aspersions on their teaching ability or on their knowledge, we must admit that we have the primary responsibility. While we are on this subject, we wonder why a body of salaried catechists could not be trained, just as is done on the foreign missions. Furthermore, we wonder why our catechisms have to be so abstract and so ponderous and why the language has to be so theological. Anyone who thinks that the children understand or retain very much of the 'religion' we teach them has only to question a class about last year's matter; the answers are informative, even if discouraging! Somehow, and soon, we must find a way to teach the truths of our Lord Jesus Christ in words and examples that modern children can understand. A good teacher can supplement the defects of the catechism, but we should still be able to provide all the teachers with a suitable manual.

Some of the blame certainly rests on the careless parents.

No one will deny that. The formation of an impressionable child is begun and completed by the parents, more than by any other influence. If the father and mother are indifferent or hostile, our efforts will, ordinarily, be counteracted, and the hope we had of forming a new Christian vanishes. Consequently we repeat that it is absolutely necessary to win over the adults of these pagan times. Without the conquest of parents, our dreams for their children are vain and bitter delusions.

But, until the parents are won over, what are we supposed to do?

We will answer the question gradually. First of all, think about our manner of teaching religion. Here, in de-Christianized cities, we act as if we were in completely Catholic surroundings; the books used are the same. If anything, the priests of the Catholic sections demand more of children who really know their Faith, while we are easier on those who know almost nothing about it. We forget that really Catholic youngsters need only to have their firm background supplemented, while the other children need a thorough grounding.

If we did go about the establishment of a catechumenate, we certainly should plan it for an age group older than our present catechism class age. Since we mean the training of the catechumenate to result in a life-dedication to the cause of Christ, it is absurd to ask such an outlook from ten- or twelve-year-olds. In the first place, they can hardly be expected to realize what we are asking of them; secondly, they are so much under the influence of their non-believing parents that our training is usually of little lasting value. By the time they are twenty-five, their only recollections of religious training are hazy notions that no one really believes; by the time their own children come along, they hand down the same unbelieving attitude, and the cycle is continued. Consequently our emphasis must be on the slightly older children who are beginning to mature. Even our best efforts towards adapting the catechism and improving the teaching of the younger boys and girls will not bring us a comparable result. Between the ages of fifteen and twenty they are beginning to realize for themselves the possibilities we are trying to uncover for them.

Bear in mind that we are not presuming to change diocesan regulations. It is a matter of speaking our minds on a subject we have observed for a long while, reaching the conclusion that the present catechism set-up produces more indifferent Christians than it does Christians. Fewer boys and girls would come to our classes if we succeeded in starting the idea of an adolescent catechumenate which would end in a more or less solemn dedication to the apostolate two years later. Despite the falling off in numbers there would be other more important gains. We firmly believe that subsequent apostasy would be decreased and that the spirit of communal Christianity would be much more firmly rooted. If our only concern is to be for numbers, we ought to resign ourselves to the present state of spiritual stagnation.

Your statements seem to be in direct contradiction to the teaching of Pius X on Children's Communions.

This objection was expected, too. In reality, there is no contradiction, because the Pope was certainly talking about children of Catholic families, and not about our neo-pagans. He meant youngsters who had grown up in religious surroundings, who had imbibed the Faith with their mother's milk, who had breathed the spirit of Christ all the days of their young lives. Surely, no one would make such a case for the spiritually undernourished children we know.

What about the sacrament of Matrimony? Surely you cannot disregard existing custom, and refuse the nuptial blessing to couples who may not be model Christians.

Unfortunately we cannot. We get cases like the young lady who came here to be married, even though she had never made her First Communion; she wanted to be married 'at church', and that was that. Another girl honestly answered 'yes' to our question about whether she believed in divorce, and we explained that it would be impossible to marry her under such a condition. The next day, her mother came in, breathing fire, and complaining about our cruelty to her daughter. We get cases similar to these every week, and they baffle and sadden us.

How can we continue to assist at the marriage of persons whom we know to be incapable of receiving the Sacrament of Matrimony?

Our Dogma and Moral Theology teach us that the validity of the Sacrament demands the intention of binding oneself before God for the rest of one's life, or at least demands the absence of a contrary intention. But what do the average couple want? The Sacrament? There is no point in pretending that they are interested in anything more than the external ceremony, the pomp and social setting. It is wrong, absolutely wrong, for us to be accomplices in this sham, and to make of one of the seven Sacraments a mere social affair. One of the worst features of the whole picture is that we priests have become servants to those who can pay for costly weddings. Later on, in our chapter on money, we will go into the question more thoroughly; it is enough to say here that our ceremonies, by some perverse twist, are more accessible to rich pagans than to poor Christians. It hurts to admit it, but everyone knows what kind of a wedding the average working girl gets, at the side altar, and as brief as possible; while a wealthy girl has the main altar, even though it often is the first time she has stepped inside the church for years.

Leaving aside the injustice of the situation, we are doing positive harm when we assist at the marriage of these neo-pagans. They do not believe in the indissolubility of marriage, and we are binding them to it! We explain the Church's position, and we put them in positive bad faith! We get them to make promises which we and they know to be lies! By the divorces which ensue we cut them off from the Christian community! Feeling the way they do, it would have been better for them—and for us—if we had let them contract a civil marriage.

In practice, how do you handle these cases?

First of all, we have to be certain that couples understand the Church's teaching on marriage; a careless explanation will not do. Usually they are so receptive at this tremendous moment of their lives that we should have little trouble. With tact and zeal we can find the proper approach. Furthermore, we ought to solemnize the marriage in proportion to the Catholicity of the prospective partners, so that the whole parish can offer prayers for their future; for indifferent Catholics, the absence of solemnity will emphasize the Christian attitude. This is a delicate matter, but one better solved by Christian principles than by money or social standing. If a couple cannot accept the Church's teaching on marriage, it is better to let them go than to take part in a practical sacrilege. Then those who do believe and those who do not will see that Christ's doctrine is a reality and not a matter of form. We will begin to 'shock' and 'startle' them with our application of what we believe.

Even if we ourselves cannot take the first practical steps in this matter, it is still a subject which should be considered by the competent authorities. Moreover, it should be weighed by every priest to whom the good of the Church is more important than personal position. Thought and prayer and *decision* are badly needed.

No doubt, you feel the same about funerals?

Even more so, because no Sacrament is involved here. As

matters stand now, the degree of honour which the official Church pays to the mortal remains of Christians is determined by money, and by nothing else. There will be more about this later, too. From the point of view of what can be done by way of example to the Christian community, there is much to comment upon. We have seen priests who were furious because lay-apostles failed to accord them the degree of respect they demanded; we have seen those same priests hold a first-class funeral for notoriously non-practising Catholics. Under those conditions, how can we honestly say that religion is a 'way of life' and not a mere business? In spite of what Canon Law says about ecclesiastical burials for public sinners, we seem to be honoured by a request for a funeral, no matter who asks us. Some of us even think that we are doing the Church a service, since another civil funeral is forestalled; we are being charitable to a poor dead sinner. Maybe so, but our charity should have started sooner, with instructions about the meaning of Christian life. Consequently we think that the funerals of sincere Christians should be as ceremonious as possible, so that the whole community may see our attitude; negligent Catholics, on the other hand, should receive a minimum of public attention.

That seems unjust, because a negligent Catholic needs prayers more than does an exemplary one.

But we are not talking about prayers, but about the pomp and ceremonies accompanying the Mass. Every deceased member of our parish has a Mass celebrated for the repose of his soul, and we remember them in special prayers. Certainly no one is going to be deprived of spiritual benefits simply because the catafalque was not the best one, or because the Mass was a low one. These additions are for the survivors, not the deceased. The purpose of the difference is to bring home to our people that the Church feels differently about loyal children.

Maybe your people will understand, but the others—the non-believers—will not, and will complain.

That statement is a revealing one. It shows that we have grown accustomed to doing unapproved, ambiguous things, simply because we lack the courage to explain the correct state of affairs to our people. We are afraid they would not understand or that they would be offended, and so we go on with unliturgical practices. Rather than do what the Church asks and what the spirit of the liturgy calls for, we prefer not to offend our people; rather than lead, we find it easier to follow. If our ceremonies are meant for those who are not Catholic and who do not understand, then there is a reason for deviations, where such deviations are allowed; but, since the Church intends her ceremonies only for her baptized children, we should keep them as they have been given to us. That is the difference between liturgy and para-liturgical functions. That is why the Church had the dismissal of catechumens in the Mass. Once a zealous lay-apostle told us that the Mass was not meant for everyone; despite the apparent heresy, she was right. Essentially, it is the assembly of Christians at prayer, offering again the Sacrifice of Calvary. It is not supposed to be the setting for a musical concert, nor the background for a public patriotic rally; those who come for the music or for the civic function only are among those for whom the Mass is meaningless. It is absurd and dangerous to expect a practical pagan to find inspiration or benefit from attendance at Mass. It is not meant for him, and his confusion or boredom is natural.

A more logical and more practical attitude is needed. We ought to distinguish between missionary liturgy and Catholic liturgy. The former will be purposely intended to draw and hold the uninitiated, while the latter will be the official worship of the signed and sealed followers of Christ. Naturally, we do not plan any police methods to ensure the Christianity of everyone who comes in the church door, but we should try to work out a programme adapted to all stages of spirituality. It is not wrong to ask people to come to church for ceremonies other than Mass. When they are present, community prayers or chant can be used in a great variety of forms, and with a great deal of profit.

One last thing in connection with this. Somehow it seems paradoxical that we should prepare children so carefully for First Communion but do almost nothing to prepare them for assistance at Mass. We insist upon their attendance at Mass, but this only leads them to think that the Mass is a pious exercise which precedes Communion, without any intrinsic connection between the two. We forget that they are catechumens, and that they need special training before they can be expected to offer the central mystery of Christianity. A child looks forward with anticipation to the day when our Lord will come to him in Holy Communion; he should, and could, also long for the day when he can join with the whole Christian community in offering the Sacrifice of the Mass.

. . . .

Foreign missioners have told us that they could never build up a living Christianity in pagan lands with the system we use at home. This is a powerful observation. Everyone knows that there are important differences between their problems and ours, but still we ought to be able to see the necessity of adopting some of their methods. To do so demands courage and ingenuity, but the prize is precious. All that we have written or shall write is done with that prize in mind.

V THE CLINK OF MONEY ROUND THE ALTAR

What would you say is the chief obstacle in your attempts to bring Christ to the people around you?

Without any hesitation we should say that it is the firmly-rooted belief that religion is nothing but a business affair. Our apologetics course, back in the seminary, made no mention of this objection; but it is by far the most powerful barrier to Christ in our day. Almost everyone believes that priests are after money, that religion is a 'racket'.

Do you think it wise to treat this question in a book intended for the general public?

We bring it up deliberately. Any lay-people who read this book will understand that we want to change this scandalous element in the life of the Church, and they will rejoice. Instead of being scandalized, they will feel relieved. After all, they are not fools; they have eyes and ears, and they know what is going on, and they are waiting for someone to be honest enough to admit our common shame. Sometimes it seems as though we priests were willing to ignore this money-abuse. The laity are not. The faithful Catholics do not complain to us, because of excessive respect for our priesthood, but they do complain among themselves about the intolerable burden they are made to bear. When we brought up this matter in discussion with lay persons here at Colombes, we could not miss the relief that was evident on their faces. At last a priest is willing to admit that this problem exists!

Some readers may fear that frankness will only serve as ammunition for the Church's enemies. The truth is that anything and everything can be used against us by those in bad faith, and we are not going to worry about that eventuality. We hope that what we are going to say here will be a proof that the priesthood is not a 'racket'. We hope that lay-apostles will be able to use this text as undeniable evidence that priests want to change the financial set-up, even to the extent of suppressing sources of revenue, so that they may be more efficient spiritual servants.

Most of those who raise this objection about money are not serious about it. It is table talk, and means nothing.

On the contrary, they are serious, and they do believe it. It does no good to tell them—even if we could—that we priests could have found more lucrative positions if our purpose in life had been the making of a fortune. The faithful realize this, but not the 'outsiders'. To the majority of men we seem to have a profitable calling, as officials in a huge organization; we are seldom now mistaken for apostles.

We say that this is a potent objection, because we have seen it as such. At every step along the road to the Church the question of money keeps cropping up. Even when a non-Catholic thinks of investigating the claims of the Church, his incipient faith is almost always killed by the unshakeable general opinion that we represent a tremendous money-making scheme, and nothing more. If a non-Catholic can withstand this overwhelmingly unanimous opinion and investigate for himself, he will see differently; but human beings do not usually oppose majorities. Everyone says that priests are interested only in money, and it must be so.

A few incidents will show you why we put so much stress on this matter of money; the examples could be multiplied easily.

I remember a house that I stopped at during one of our district missions. The woman who opened the door did not even give me a chance to say why I was there; she immediately said that she had already contributed. To my shame she said it loud enough for passers-by to hear. That was how zeal for Christ was mistaken; I was trying to speak the word of God, and she was answering 'money'. Standing there on the door-step, I convinced her that I had not come for a collection, and she let me come in; before long the message of Christ had touched her heart, and she said she would come to the mission. Despite the fact that I had expressly told her that money was not my object, and despite the fact that we had been talking only about religious matters, she tried to force some money on me as I was leaving. The connection between priests and money was deeply rooted. She insisted that I take it, 'for the poor'; I told her that she could do that directly herself, and went off, leaving the good woman in her astonishment.

Another stop was at the flat of an old couple who had been away from church since they left their country home. It was fairly easy to get them to promise that they would come to some of the services, but I noticed that they were exchanging embarrassed looks while I was talking. Finally, the old lady let it be known that they were not able to afford to give much, because the pension they received was just enough to live on. When I explained, emphatically, that no money was expected, that no special clothes were required, the relief on their faces was good to see!

How do you account for the fact that this prejudice is so widespread?

Good Lord, put yourself in the position of an ordinary working-man! Of the few contacts he has with priests, very few do not involve money; it is almost inevitable that he should come to consider religion as a financial question. We never demand money for Baptism, but a contribution is certainly expected. We never demand payment for preparing children for First Communion, but the seats in church are paid for on that great day, and the candles the children hold have to be paid for—and returned to the sacristy after the ceremony. The clothes the children wear accentuate the difference between the rich and the poor. None of this is simoniacal, and, in fact, none of the money usually goes to the priest himself. However, it appears to, and the ordinary person will not make any investigation or distinctions; as far as he is concerned the priest gets the money, and that is that.

When working-people are married, do you think that they are blind to the class distinctions we foster or permit? For those who can afford them, we furnish a bedecked high altar, music, carpets; for those who cannot, the side altars and silent plainness are good enough. Can we blame them for their bitterness and their cynicism? We try to tell them that the Sacrament is the same, and that all these external trappings mean nothing; they ask us why we permit and receive payment for what we say is 'vanity'. They ask us how we can preach our Lord's words about wealth, how we can say his 'Blessed are the poor'. We can talk all we want, and make as many distinctions as we want, but the evident facts are against us. In religion, as in everything else, you pay for what you get.

Ironically enough we cannot hope to become rich on these tiny sources of revenue; we have acquired a reputation, but not wealth. Still, it is that name, that stigma, which is blocking our efforts to bring Christ to our world. The clink of money round his altar makes it impossible to hear his words.

Funerals are a good example of the inequality you mentioned.

Unfortunately they are. We have to admit it. Even when a person is dead, his money (or lack of it) determines the honour which the official Church is willing to grant her child. We have a regular scale of prices for different kinds of Requiem Masses; sometimes those who cannot meet even the lowest price have to be content with the priest's blessing! Even in the hour of their death we consecrated ministers of God deny to his children what he most certainly intends them to have. Part of the fault lies in the fact that we have stepped into the background, and have let funeral directors arrange matters with the bereaved families. Nowadays the undertaker sees the family, finds out what kind of a Mass they want, and tells them how much it will cost. We have permitted this important part of a person's life to become a mere business transaction—so much Christian worship for so much money. Naturally, our people are bitter about it.

The shameful part of all this is that everyone considers it as normal. Those who can pay for honours will receive them; those who cannot will not. That is the rule. What a tragedy! What a travesty of the teaching and the life of Christ, whose followers we claim to be! And yet we have to admit that the Church has adopted secular standards, in practice, until the stage has been reached where wealth buys this honour which belongs only to those who earned it by their Christian lives. We ought to thank God that he cannot become hypocritical, as we do; he searches the heart of man, and knows each of us for what we are. We tell the people that God is merciful, and that he will apply the merits of Christ where they are needed, but it takes a great deal of faith for anyone to see that we *believe* that. According to the way we act, the Solemn High Mass for the rich man is more efficacious than the simple absolution we give a pauper. What are our people to believe?

Usually these class distinctions are made on account of merely external trappings. Is it not just that those who want them should have to pay for them?

It is meet and just; they cost money and they must be paid for. Even a working-family could pay for them, because their wedding receptions, for example, cost twenty times as much as the Church fee which they complain about. But, here, we are not worried about what is just or legal; we are concerned, like St Paul, about what is expedient. The mission cause is at stake in little things like these. If we are going to give scandal, let it be the kind of scandal Christ gave when he consorted with sinners and the publicans; at least, let us stop the opposite scandal, which our present attitude about money is giving. Because the world seems to have lost the idea of selfless service of others, we ought to give proof that the Church and ministers of Christ are here for just that reason. Because the modern world believes that 'you pay for what you get', we ought to show them that their principle does not hold true in the Catholic Church. We are not after tips; we are after their souls.

It is bad enough for a priest to live in luxury, and to enjoy personal comforts which the vast majority of his flock cannot afford. But it is worse, far worse, for him to expose the gifts of God which he administers to scorn and cynical contempt, simply because he practically demands money for them. We are not tradesmen, and it is time we stopped acting like tradesmen. Until the world sees that we are servants of Christ, with proof from our attitude towards money, they will laugh at our apostolic schemes. And it would be difficult to blame them.

You seem to say that our present system of collections and seat money is unjustifiable.

Taking things as they are, we say that no one who believed that priests were obsessed by money would find any reason for changing his mind were he to attend a church service of any kind. The collection (or collections) begins at the *Credo* and lasts till the Communion; it is taken up by priests who might better be occupied in helping the people to attend Mass intelligently; it is preceded by a sermon composed of lengthy appeals for a thousand different parish needs. Small wonder that people think as they do about us.

One afternoon I was out walking with a friend of mine. Even though he was indifferent about religion, he remarked that the church we were passing was the parish church of his childhood, and he spoke of all the memories it brought back to him. Naturally I seized the opportunity and persuaded him to drop in for a visit—his first visit to a church for many years. We were hardly inside the door when an usher sidled up to us and whispered 'Ten cents'. Without taking him too seriously, I whispered back that we had dropped in for a moment only. His voice became more stern as he informed us that he was not concerned about the length of our visit; the price was ten cents. My friend had been standing by during this conversation, near an old priest who was walking up and down, saying his Breviary and oblivious to all the commotion. This was too much for a man who had lost the Faith, and he turned to me and said, 'Let's get out of here. This trafficking is shameful, and it is always like this'. My ears burned at that last phrase, at the terrible condemnation it contained; and I thought with sorrow of all the men and women of good will who are being kept away from Christ because of petty scandals like this.

What do we think our people are? Week in and week out we preach money to them—appeals for the Holy Childhood, for the school, for fuel, for everything. We are not saying that these are not worthy causes, but we are saying that we ought to give our people a rest, and permit them to hear the untainted word of God. A sentence or two can tell them about the nature of an ordinary appeal, and we can devote most of the sermon-time to the sermon.

Besides the financial sermons, we disgust our faithful with the custom of paying for seats in the house of God. They come to pray, to worship God, and we take advantage of their love of God to collect a few more cents. True, the money is not intended for our pockets, but that is not the point. True, the money may be needed, but that is not the point either. We are talking about the ceaseless and irritating demands for money; regardless of their purpose or their need, they do estrange our people. They are a scandal and a stumbling block, and should be treated as such. Ask any lay apostle what he or she says when they are taunted with the charge that the Church is a business organization. Try to think of an answer which would satisfy a non-believer who saw with his own eyes, and not the eyes of Faith, what was going on every day in almost every Catholic church in the land. Honestly and frankly, how can we expect a pagan world to believe that we are apostles with a supernatural commission?

You are talking childishly. Do you think priests like to keep on asking for money? Do you think that the parish is going to live on hot air? Our work demands money, and how shall we get it if we do not ask for it?

We realize that priests hate to be forever begging, and we realize that parish needs are always pressing. Just as in other points of this book, we are not laying any claim to have found the solution of a torturing dilemma. We are not setting ourselves up as models to be followed; like many, many others, we are trying to find an answer to this perplexing problem of money. Moreover, all our observations are made from the perspective of priests engaged in the conversion of a semi-pagan parish; they will not, consequently, apply as aptly to a parish of true Christians. It is a difficulty we all face, to a greater or lesser degree, and we can only hope that our words will be taken (as they are meant) in a spirit of fraternal and constructive criticism.

In practice, we try to keep two aims in view. One is to reduce as far as possible the amount of money we need; the other is to regulate our use of the money so as to dissipate any prejudice about priests and money which may be lurking in the minds of our own parishioners. If you recall what we said about parish activities, you will remember that one of our objections to them was that they cost too much for the results they obtained; also they make us appear wealthy, even though we are far from that. Hence we favoured the direct apostolate, both for economy and for results. Even for that we need money, of course; but it is much less, and can be raised without perpetual appeals or parish bazaars.

Usually spontaneous gifts take care of our budget for the ceremonies and literature, and a few wealthy persons can always be approached in case of real need.

Before going on to the six principles about money which we, with deference to better ideas, are going to enumerate, we should like to point out two errors which a great many priests commit.

One is in connection with building. Frankly, it seems that some parish priests have a passion for building; churches, schools, parish halls, trail in their wake as they move from parish to parish. Some of them are needed, but more of them are the fruit of personal pride. And what happens? The parish is burdened with a debt for years to come, and the endless cycle of appeals for money is put in motion. Besides that, many of the buildings become completely useless, as our city population moves around. It would be far wiser to restrain the building impulse until a case of actual need arises, and thus to spare the people a heavy debt and a legacy of ill-feeling between the parish and its future priests. Just in passing, I should like to quote a witticism made by a priest-friend of mine. We were being shown through a new hall which one of these 'building fathers' had just erected, and my companion, after remarking about how well it had been built, how spacious it was, etc., said 'Now all you have to do is fill it'.

The second error is the belief that, because we actually do expend most of our income on charitable causes, we are helping to break down the prejudice we have been describing. As we mentioned in the section of charitable activities, such is normally not the case. Understandably, the recipients of our charity get the idea that we must be very wealthy, and a city population, especially, has no compunction about relieving us of a part of it. This is not to say that we should put an end to our charity. We simply want to clarify the point of view of those who think that, because we help with the money we receive, people will therefore understand why we ask for money. It is not as easy as all that.

Granting all that, we still should like to hear your six suggestions.
Here they are then. Just as everything else we have written or shall write, they are subject to the official decision

of the hierarchy, which is in a far better position to see the whole picture than we are.

1. Talk less often about money from the pulpit. The congregation have come to hear the doctrine of Christ. If we let it be known that we shall deliberately refrain from the subject of finance, we can be certain that they will give more generously than they did for our long-winded appeals.

2. Never give the impression that money is of primary importance in the advance of the Kingdom of God. Our priestly purpose must never be swayed one way or another, simply because the one we are called upon to serve is rich or poor.

3. If possible, do away with seat-money. Here at Colombes we have a quarterly collection for that purpose, and everyone seems pleased with the elimination of the weekly unpleasantness. At the evening services that we described in the section on liturgy, there is never a collection for any reason.

4. Have as few collections as possible, and make them as inconspicuous as possible. At Mass, the Offertory collection is a part of the liturgy, properly understood, and it should be kept in that sense. Never prolong it. To help show its connection with the Mass, one pastor whom I know has the baskets placed upon the altar during the rest of the Sacrifice. Outside of Mass we never take up a collection; it is wrong to capitalize on the goodness of our people every time they step inside the church door.

Some priests will say that such an attitude towards money is idealistic; like a pastor I know, they are firm believers in the old system where the parish priests pass the basket with a knowing eye on every member of the congregation. To such we can only say that a deeper trust in the providence of God is never displeasing to him. Let us tell you an incident that happened to us; it is not a 'miracle-story', but it does demonstrate what we mean. Five years ago we decided to do away with the traditional seat-money and candle-offering that goes with First Communion. After we had taken the resolution our faith wavered; thinking of our parish budget and the disastrous consequences our foolhardy step would have upon it, we asked God for a sign that we

were doing the right thing. Just as he did for the weak
Israelites in the desert, he did for us; within a few days two
unexpected and anonymous gifts of considerable size came
to us. Since then similar incidents have occurred again and
again. Knowing that our parishioners are far from making
a habit of this sort of thing, we marvel and we thank God.
To some these happenings may not provide any evidence
of any connection between our plans and God's pleasure;
we can only believe that they do.

5. Eliminate as far as possible the distinctions now in
vogue at weddings and funerals. Show, by word and deed,
that we do not look upon these occasions as sources of
revenue. Make a real effort to enter into the joy or the
sorrow of those who come to arrange matters with us, so
that they can see in us their priest and not an official of
some organization. Talk to them about the Sacrament they
are going to receive or the help they can give the deceased
by their prayers; keep away from every reference to money.
Many of the present differences will disappear when our
ideal of a united and praying community is realized.

6. Put charitable activities in the hands of lay-apostles.
That will rid our people of the false notion that we are
inexhaustibly wealthy; also it will make for more efficiency
in the distribution of charity, and will cause our laity to be
active in this important part of Christianity.

*Have you anything to say about the practice of personal poverty
on the part of the clergy?*

That was a rhetorical question, we are sure. As a matter
of fact, poverty is the most telling proof of the Gospel we
preach; unlike our personal chastity, our poverty can be
demonstrated. It will prove that we have left all things to
follow Christ, and that he is sufficient for us. Many a priest
does give this testimony, especially in rural areas, but it is
by no means universal. Often our failure in this regard is
not due to avarice, but to a lack of understanding about
the power of this proof, and to a forgetting of what we are.
And even when we are not rich, but simply comfortable,
we do not realize that our standard of living is superior to
many of our parishioners; our furnishings and table and
pleasures are out of the reach of their income. In itself that

is not necessarily evil, but neither is it good when it results in a feeling that they are 'beneath' the man who was ordained to serve and guide them. Sometimes it is a mixed blessing never to have known want or hunger. For one thing it makes it difficult for a priest to tell his parishioners to bear their sufferings patiently, when they are hungry or out of work, and he is well-fed and has money in his pocket. It makes it difficult to go into homes where your parishioners are cold and ill-clothed and try to tell them of God's love for those who bear crosses patiently, when their eyes tell you that they know you are warm and well clothed.

All of this may sound harsh. We know that many of our confrères do not fall into this category, because they do know what want is, and they do give of their very sustenance to those who are poor and hungry and naked. We also know that many do not. Think what it means to live in insecurity, to be uncertain about next week's food and rent and clothing. Realize that that is the ordinary lot of most of our working-class parishioners. Then think about our own lives and our own security, and we shall see what a gulf there is between our people and us, even when we are far from wealthy ourselves. By gradual, unconscious steps, we grow into a state of mind which looks for personal security more than for apostolic results. Even our clerical parlance betrays us, for when we speak of a 'good parish', we mean one which provides a good living for its clergy; when we talk about promotion in the ranks of the clergy, we mean that the priest in question has gone to a wealthier parish. Something is wrong.

In any case, the result is that we have no close sympathy with our people, nor they with us. We cannot even hope to have the irresistible influence of the Apostles, of St Martin of Tours, of St Francis, of the Curé of Ars. In our churches there is heard the clink of money round the altar.

VI CLERICAL CULTURE

Surely you are not going to say that our culture is an obstacle to the evangelization of our people?

Strange though it may sound, we do say that. It will take a great deal of explaining before you will see what we mean, but we shall do our best to prove our point. Lest you cite examples like Abbé Godin, who was certainly a cultured man, and who yet succeeded remarkably in his apostolate among people who were far from refined, we say that he succeeded because he knew how to overcome his own gentility.

Please explain what you mean.

We mean that our influence upon ordinary people is not what it should be, partly because we are so different from them; we think differently, live differently, speak and act differently. In other words, we have a different culture. Our seminary training in the classics, philosophy and theology has put us in a class apart. Properly speaking, we are not like *any* of our parishioners, but we seem more 'middle-class' or 'bourgeois' than anything else. What is the result? Usually it means that we feel compelled to surround ourselves with those who will understand our thought and our speech, and who have tastes like our own. One of the reasons for the rise of the 'parish atmosphere' we spoke of at the beginning of this book is found in the priests; we tend to move among and work with people who resemble us—it is easy to do so. In fact, it is wise; that is the basic principle of Catholic Action expressed in the formula of 'like to like'. Our objection comes from the consequent forgetfulness of the great mass of men who are not like us. Our concern is about the consequent inability to meet ordinary people, to talk to them, to make them feel at home in the 'catholic' Church we represent. Even when we do attempt to make contact with them, we use terminology which is completely foreign to the ordinary working-man; more than that, we take for granted the fact that they already accept the basic ideas of Christianity, even though they do not. What we are trying to say to them goes against every principle of modern pagan life, and yet we blissfully assume the very things we must prove and demonstrate. We are living in another world, a tidy clerical and philosophical world. It is time to come down to earth!

But is our culture so completely foreign to the average working man?

Our answer is an unqualified 'yes'. If anybody wants to debate whether or not he is capable of absorbing it, that is another matter. However, as things are now, we say that our culture is completely foreign to him, so much so that he distrusts it. Briefly we will outline some of the more obvious differences between our world and his.

Cultured or educated men reason out their actions, and they live by a set of principles which their intellect has come to adopt. Ordinary men, on the other hand, act through sentiment or through principles accepted by their neighbours; most of their rules of action can be reduced to eminently practical and completely materialistic proverbs. Everyone has heard them. 'Make hay while the sun shines'. 'Make the most of a good thing while you have it.' 'If you don't take care of yourself, who will?' The same thing can be seen in the usual attitude of parents when their child tells them that he was in a fight at school; the first question is always whether or not he fought back, because the greatest shame of all is to let someone else take advantage of one.

Another difference is in the critical spirit of educated men. They will discuss and dissect whatever is proposed to them, sometimes simply because they are unwilling, in principle, to follow the herd. Again, the mass of men are quite the opposite. They take as their own the opinion of the majority, and they act collectively upon that opinion. This is not the result of a lack of personal courage, but, rather, a poverty of ideas; it is not so much an unwillingness to find objective truth as it is satisfaction with the ideas which their own milieu has provided ready made for them. Personality is swallowed up in the group. Such men will be firm enough in expressing their opinions, but they fail to realize that their conclusions are not really their own.

Cultured men base their judgements on certain criteria outside themselves, but the ordinary working-man's standard is less exacting; generally he is satisfied with the creed which begins: 'it's all a matter of opinion'. Since schooldays he has heard innumerable contradictions of every fact and dogma under the sun; radio, films and magazines pour over him more confusion than he can handle. Consequently a knowing cynicism becomes his practical philosophy of life, and even his power of judgement is swallowed up in the common attitude of his class.

You sound like one of these superior sociologists who say that the 'Labouring Classes' are incapable of thought.

We do not mean to, because we are not sociologists and we definitely do not feel superior to the working-class. At the beginning of this book we touched upon this whole subject; we said that, until they have begun to find themselves again in their family circle, the majority of workers would not think for themselves. That was why we stressed the importance of group-apostolates, and the importance of family life. Our cities do something to a person; they strip him of his individualism and personality, principally because they make normal family life so difficult. Hence we must help them to find themselves, their traditions, their self-respect and honesty, by trying to restore that family unit. Then they will think and act from principle rather than from group-compulsion.

What would you consider as the cause of our radical difference from our people?

One of the main causes is certainly our theological training. We need it, of course, and need it badly; we are supposed to know as much as possible about the mysteries of God, his ways and his plans. Without that knowledge we cannot lead others to him, since the blind cannot lead the blind. However, we have learned it bookishly, not vitally; we have left it in its intellectual dress, and have not made it a part of our lives. Our highbrow attitude about the things of God is alien both to our people and to the Gospel we are supposed to preach, and we are failing both. We think that people are rejecting Christ when, often, they are rejecting only our bloodless and unreal presentation of him. Our talks and sermons may be chiselled to grammatical perfection and formed from the most orthodox of

sources, but they mean nothing to our hearers. We need
the gift of tongues. Besides that, we need the ability to
listen, and to let others talk to us about their spiritual
discoveries; we may and should know more about theology
than our parishioners do, but many of them could teach us
about God and about how to present him to our flock.

That is one of the best features of the study-clubs—everyone gets a chance to talk, and then we are forced to listen.
The effect is good for them and for us. It is much more
real to hear a man or woman tell about his or her contact
with God than it is to listen to a logical, but unreal, talk
based upon a scholastic syllogism.

Someone told us once about an English priest who brings
the daily paper into the pulpit, reads some article to the
people, and proceeds from there to a Christian demonstration of the subject. No doubt he scandalizes a great many
parishioners. Scandal or not, he is more attuned to the
needs of the times than are those super-scholastics who get
up to talk about the Omnipresence of God, for example,
and who start: 'My friends, God is everywhere, by his
Presence, his Essence, his Power. First, by his Essence . . .'.
Christ did not talk like a scholar. He was of the people and
among the people and his language and metaphors and
examples are immortal in their appeal to the common man.
He, who is God, knew that the humdrum affairs of everyday
life are what every man knows and what every man must
learn how to use in his approach to God.

If we wish to make a show of our great knowledge, the
congregation cannot prevent us; neither can they assimilate
what we are trying to say. When we soar, we soar alone.
The average person is more interested in the fact of Christ's
presence in the Eucharist, for example, than he is in the
mode of that presence. The same is true for all the tremendous dogmas of our Faith. Our people are eager to be able
to put them into practice—in the life which God has given
them to lead; the historical and philosophical background
of these truths does not interest them. Most Catholics are
unconcerned about their inability to answer objections made
by unbelievers, but they are concerned about their own
service of Christ. Before an intellectual, reflective audience,

our technique would change, naturally, but it is the height of folly to suppose that such an audience is the usual thing. Most men want an external expression of their internal faith, and our cold presentation frustrates them. We might as well learn now to accept and use human nature as it is. If we doubt whether man can live by rational bread alone, the success of innumerable public expressions of faith should convince us. At some of them, here in France, the most indifferent and anti-religious souls have been moved to return to Christ, and we are not a peculiar people in this regard; the same principle underlies our liturgy, all our shrines and pilgrimages. And yet, Sunday morning sees us treating these same souls as though they were angels and not men.

One winter we held a study club on the 'Our Father'. It was easy to see that the study made far less impression than did the attempts to reduce the meaning of our Lord's prayer to the scenes and problems of their own lives. That was what they needed, and that was what they did.

In your efforts to escape formalism in religion, you are running the obviously equal danger of de-spiritualizing it.

A very true observation. We do have to be careful, because we can be misunderstood and give occasion for superstition. As a matter of fact, that tendency was responsible, to some extent, for the success of our experiment with the passing of the statue of the Blessed Mother, which we described in a previous chapter. Some families took part in it simply because they felt it would be unlucky to break the chain. What can you do? We see the danger, and we try to be sensible in our material approach to religion; it would be absurd to shy off from it altogether, just because of the possibility of its abuse. For every external act of devotion there must be a corresponding explanation of the interior meaning. Since we are body and soul, and the soul cannot be reached directly, the material side of man must be the approach to the soul, and we make every effort to use such an approach. Superstition is one extreme to be avoided, and disembodied, intellectual spirituality is the other. We have tried to find the middle course.

What do you think about the literary tastes of priests?

If they are an obstacle to our ability to bring Christ to his people, we say 'Get rid of them'. When we try to present him to uneducated audiences in language and phrases and literary devices that we borrow from the 'great' books we read, we are wasting our time as well as the people's. Our subtleties of style are lost on them. This sounds very harsh, we know; if the Gospels were not so simple and matter-of-fact, we should hesitate to advance this opinion. But, with Christ on our side, we feel more sure. His audience was much like our own, and we can see how he talked to them.

Honestly, it is hard to follow you. Do you mean to say that the good education we have received must be considered as a stumbling block to our apostolic work?

Of course not. We warned you that this question was a difficult one to understand and to explain. When we cry out against 'clerical culture' we mean the way in which priests tend to make use of their training. We do not seem to realize that everything we learned and absorbed was meant for the souls among whom we would labour; instead of that, it has become clerical property. When we give it out, its dress is clerical, and its wording, and its meaning. A 'class' culture has arisen, even though that is contrary to our very purpose in life. Even our manners are so very different from those of other good Christians that they have come to be caricatured by the term 'churchy manners' —meaning a mixture of unction, pomposity and caution. That is why we object to our education, or rather, to its results.

It need not be so. We can be educated to the finger-tips, capable of appreciating art and music and letters, and yet be simple, approachable men. There are plenty of proofs of that in the ranks of the clergy. Until we shake off that unwarranted dignity, our work will suffer. There is no reason in the world why a priest cannot strive for the real, unalloyed dignity of his calling as a fisher of men, and learn how to adapt himself to the code of his people. Instead of being offended that a man should presume to talk to us with his hat on, or with a cigarette in his mouth, we should realize that no offence is implied in these acts, according to the social laws of the man's circle. Instead of being mortified when someone shouts a greeting and carries on a conversation with us from the other side of the street, we should be able to see that friendliness, and not contempt, is being shown. Our 'churchy outlook' on life needs over-hauling.

We are different, and should remain so, but the difference is far more spiritual than material—or should be. When we preserve this difference by clerical pomposity, we are wrong; when we try to rid ourselves of it by being patronizing or by being too much like a lay-person, we are equally wrong. The balance is found in a burning love of Christ, which expresses itself in unaffected simplicity, solely because we love these people whom he has given us to lead to him; any other, forced, simplicity is a sham, and will be quickly seen as such, for our people are keen judges of their fellow-men. This is the balance which Don Bosco found, and the Curé of Ars, and countless other priests of Jesus Christ. This is the balance St Paul defined in the Epistle to the Hebrews, when he said that a priest was a man 'taken from among men, and ordained for men in those things which have to do with the service of God'. Because of this passion to bring Christ to the working-classes, whose loss we lament, some priests, like Father Loew in Marseilles, have even begun to labour with their hands at the docks and in the mines. Even though some may consider this an extreme, it is, at least, a testimony to heroic priestliness; it may prove to be a very practical, and even necessary, part of the training of future apostles to the working-class.

Are there any other obstacles?

Yes, indeed. One would be our personal likes and dis-likes, in so far as they are carried into our priestly work. We are not so lacking in understanding of human nature as to think that we can ever rid ourselves completely of these personal preferences, but they must not be left un-checked. When they make us avoid certain people, or make certain people avoid us, they are a definite obstacle. As much as possible we must try to be all things to all men, so as not to hurt and alienate other human beings. We are priests, and we are ordained for all men, not just for those we like. People are sensitive before us partly because they realize, dimly or clearly, our exalted office, and partly because they feel inferior to us in one way or another. Learn their likes and dislikes, and then make use of them honestly, for the cause of Christ. Forgive this personal note, but it is such a striking proof of the perception of our people when they see that a priest loves them unashamedly, that I feel obliged to tell it. One Christmas Eve, at Midnight Mass, a curate overheard two working-men at the end of the sermon I had just preached on Christ's love for the poor. One of them said to the other 'He is one of our own, that priest!' Ignoring the fact that the compliment was a personal one, it does show what we mean. When we actually do love them all, they sense it, and respond to it; we become, as we should be, an avenue to Christ. When we permit personal caprice to direct our apostolate we become obstacles.

Yet we are supposed to be leaders. You seem to say that we should be merely friends and helpers.

Remember that we are working among non-Catholics who have no reason for following us; it is utter folly to consider oneself as a 'leader' in their eyes. Unlike the Pope and the Bishops we have no *ex cathedra* authority, even over our own faithful flock; we, like them, follow the directives of the hierarchy. What power we have should be used sparingly, because the dictatorial attitude affected by some priests is an intolerably obnoxious quality. It is more in keeping with the office of a priest to draw his flock to love the same divine things which he loves, to influence and attract them to the beauty of Almighty God. To some this will sound like weakness. If it meant that we were to be benevolent in a sickly fashion, if it meant that we were to utter nothing but platitudes, if it meant that we must avoid hurting anybody's feelings—then we would agree. It is none of these things. We do have a commission to preach, and that assignment necessitates telling the truth; we do not intend to advocate anything less than that. But there are various ways of fulfilling that commission. To our mind harsh words and bitter tongue-lashings are not the way of Jesus Christ, any more than the other extreme of colourless, watered Christianity is. One who loves his people will understand how hard it is for them to fulfil the duties of their state in life, and will try to help them find the most practical means of doing it; he will not shout at them, nor will he lay down a penal code of fire and brimstone.

We must enter into the hearts and minds of our people, so as to be able to convince them that the law of God is really for their own good; and even though difficult to fulfil, he will help us all to comply with it. This is not weakness, unless love be weakness. If so, we do not know what to answer to our Lord, who said: 'You know that those who are regarded as rulers among the Gentiles lord it over them, and their great men exercise authority over them. *But it is not so among you.* On the contrary, whoever wishes to become great shall be your servant; and whoever wishes to be first among you shall be the slave of all; for the Son of Man also has not come to be served, but to serve, and to give his life as a ransom for many.' And what will you answer to our Lord, since he said to all of us that he would no longer call us servants, but friends? Even the communists know this much. Their leaders are 'comrades', and great care is taken that their popularity be preserved, and their identity with the struggling masses be never obscured. We priests of God seem to have forgotten both the command of Christ and the psychology of human beings.

Part of the reason for this is, as we said before, the natural result of our training. We are separated from ordinary people during all the years of our intellectual and cultural grooming; when we emerge, it is into a strange and crude world. Naturally we tend to avoid crudeness and to move in the circle most like the delicate cocoon which hatched us. Unfortunately a priest cannot afford to act 'naturally'. We must—and it is impossible to over-emphasize this—go out to the ordinary people, mix with them, know their wants and hopes and feelings, love them, and thus bring them back to Christ who died for just such as these. They may not be as polite as we think they should be; they may be ignorant and prejudiced and ungrateful; they may even be unwashed, noisy, and vulgar. These are the ones whom we avoid and who avoid us—but no more! They may be less obviously unpleasing, and be simply smug middle-class bores but these, too, are woefully in need of Christ. We must stop limiting the Kingdom of God until it includes only those who resemble us; we are meant to love all men without exception. It is hard, dreadfully hard, to love without sham and without reserve, when the beloved is so unappealing. It takes sanctity, and sanctity of a special kind. Despite the prevailing attitude, priests are not exempt from the obligation of acquiring that sanctity, that heart of Jesus Christ.

You reduce the difficulty to the fact that we have let our culture make us strangers to our own people. Is that correct?

Precisely. Our conversation, our manner of thinking, our choice of friends are alien to the common understanding and the common good of the parish as a whole. The natural preferences we give free rein to, colour our sermons, make our choice of examples, determine what families we visit. A dangerous road for a priest to follow! Our priestly influence becomes narrower, and our priestly hearts become less catholic. Simultaneously those outside the Church are given a false picture of her; they naturally come to believe that she is interested in the churchgoers only, and not in the spiritual 'down-and-outs'.

The niceties of polite society are not to be scorned, but neither are they to be confused with the essence of Christianity. This whole problem is a more profound one than mere concern with social conventions in the life of a priest, but these do illustrate, concretely, what is meant by our statement that we have become strangers to the working-class members of our flock. The heart of the difficulty lies in this, that we have enclosed ourselves in our own little clerical world, and that we have tried to make the outside world conform to that pattern. If it will not, we avoid contact with it; if it will, we feel that we are accomplishing something. The truth is that we have failed in the rôle of an 'alter Christus' and are playing the part of an 'alter ego', dressed in clerical robes.

Would you expand a little some of the passing references you made to the subject of sermons?

We would not miss this chance for the world. The special feature of sermons, as far as we are concerned here, is the problem of adaptation to the audience before us; like so many other difficulties brought up in this book, it is easy to talk about, but very hard to solve. For example, I listened to two sermons on the subject of 'The Fatherhood of God', given by two of the newly-ordained curates here. Both were zealous, aware of the need for adaptation; but neither of the talks fitted the audience in that church. One of the priests compared God to our earthly father, rising from earthly love and solicitude to the divine; the other described the death of his own father with telling emotion, and drew his lesson from the loss he experienced. These were good sermons, even excellent ones—but, I repeat, they were not adapted to our parishioners. During the sermons my gaze wandered around the church, and I saw a girl whose father had driven her from the house, and told her to earn her living on the sidewalks, the way her mother had done. I saw another girl whose father perpetually abused the girl's mother. Do you see what I mean? If those young preachers had known the difference between the world in which they had been brought up, and the world in which these people live, they would never have used that approach to the fatherhood of God. These young workers, generally speaking, have no consciousness of pride and love for their parents, because they so often have no reason for love or pride in them, at least not along the lines pointed out by the priest in the pulpit. For this audience the talk was unreal, romantic, even fantastic.

Do you receive any criticisms of the sermons from parishioners?

Very many, especially since we deliberately encourage them to let us know how the sermons affected them. There is hardly any better way to find out how to preach to this particular audience. From what they tell us we know that they sense when a sermon is poorly or hurriedly prepared; when sincerity is lacking, when a preacher is more interested in fine phrasing than in Christ's doctrine. One thing especially striking is the comment that the Gospel itself is often easier to understand than the preacher's explanation of it! The people tell us about words or expressions which we are always using without realizing our fault, and which detract from the force of our message. All of these things are told in a spirit of mutual charity, from a desire to help and to be helped. There is nothing unkind or sarcastic

141

about them. As a matter of fact it is a marvellous advantage to have them tell us what they think. Most congregations have no chance to express their minds, and so they sleep all through the sermon, lulled by the drone of our voices and by the unreal truisms we are mouthing. And yet we have a divine commission to preach the Word of God! To us is given the task which the Apostles began! We are indeed unprofitable servants when that glorious task is carried out hurriedly, insincerely, verbosely or professorially.

Too often it happens, as we have seen and heard, that the Sunday sermon is a tissue of magnificent words which no longer mean anything to the people. They will understand the words, of course, but the meaning, the background, the implications are lost on them, no matter how well known these same expressions may be to the seminary-trained preacher. The meat of the sermon is missing. When the people go home they bring with them no nourishment for a week of work and problems in this present world. What they heard may have been beautiful, but it was as useful as a description of some Roman ruins. One writer compared the contents of the usual sermon to the vestments that the priests wear at Mass; they are used only at Mass, and then put away and forgotten until the next religious service. A bitter comparison, but not an untrue one.

Where is the familiar, powerful language of the Fathers of the Church? Why are we so unlike them? One reason is that we are afraid of offending our people; we feel sure that they would take offence, and depart, never to return. We might well be wrong about that, but, even if some did leave, we firmly believe that many more would come in, to find out what Christ is saying to our day and age. Another, and more fundamental, reason is that *we think we are talking to men and women who already are real Christians*. Hence we use Scriptural quotations, theological terminology and scientifically exact Christian language. We sound eloquent. We are orthodox. Most of all, we are satisfied with our sermon. As we come down from the pulpit, and the thought crosses our mind that what we have said will not change our people very much, we brush away the misgivings; either the Devil is trying to ensnare us or else these people are incapable of grasping the majestic heights of Christian revelation. Next week we go through the same process and the same misgivings, and the week after that, year in and year out.

Somehow it seldom occurs to us that the fault may be ours, and not theirs. We would realize that, and we would say 'mea culpa', if we would but stop for a moment and consider the souls who are listening to us. Certainly we should know by now that most of them have little or no religious background, less knowledge of doctrine, and still less familiarity with our theological vocabulary. Having grasped that, we would mount the pulpit in a different frame of mind and with a different approach. We would be changed men, and so would our people be. With stereotyped phrases abandoned, the awful truth of Christianity would stand revealed to these people, perhaps for the first time; with Christianity presented according to their present problems they would find the answer to the doubts that gnaw at the souls of those whom we now think of as 'Christian'.

One possible way to get that proper approach is to realize that we are talking to neophytes, to catechumens, to pagans who simply happened to drop into Mass. One priest told us about the comment that a non-believing friend of his made, after he had heard his priest-friend preach at a parish mission. He told him that the sermon had been well delivered, but that it was obvious that the priest had intended to talk to people who were already convinced about the truth of Christianity—and only to them. He went on to say that if the church had been filled with men and women in his frame of mind, the sermon would have been useless.

We are not trying to say that every time a priest gets up to preach he should talk only on the ABCs of religion, and that in the most simple manner. Evidently there is need of progression, especially during a mission or even in a series of parish sermons. We do, however, mean that a priest will be much more effective if he is constantly aware of the necessity of speaking to those who know little and believe less about Christianity. Instead of taking for granted that everyone in the congregation is a firm believer, he will remember those whose faith is weak or lost. Instead of assuming that the congregation can follow and understand his technical Christian concepts, he will remember those who sit in darkness, even in these Christian countries of ours. Instead of presenting Christ's doctrine as a completely spiritual and unworldly matter, he will try to reach out to these souls by being more realistic, more concrete.

It certainly should not be difficult to be concrete in preaching.

But it is. It could be easier, if we would but remember certain principles, like the following. Keep in mind that we are talking, not to an 'audience', but to men and women of flesh and blood, with particular and pressing problems of daily life. Keep in mind that 'suffering' and 'evil' are not abstract terms to them, but that these words have a definite, actual and personal association. Remember that 'love' calls to their minds concrete persons, and individual longings; that 'justice' has a vivid connection with their jobs; that the 'destiny of mankind' means the longfelt answer to the confusion and helplessness of men and women in this modern age.

Realization of the intimate connection which must exist between what we say and to whom we are saying it will keep us from much of the pompous, meaningless verbiage which is the scourge of our apostolate in the pulpit. For every priest and for every parish, the needs, and the consequent adaptations, will be different; by trial and by prayer, and by common sense, we shall find our own proper approach. Unless we make that effort we shall go on with our torrent of words, signifying nothing. Our responsibility is overwhelming. We are the only ones in the whole of God's world who can give a meaning to life, who can answer the torturing doubts and despair of the confused twentieth century; without the message of Christ which we were ordained to spread, nothing can halt the growth of self-destruction. We must do it, for no one else can. In order to do it, we must be truly apostolic. We must be apostolic preachers. If we speak the word of God from routine, or because we were assigned to preach on this particular Sunday, we are failures. If we speak that word merely to hear ourselves talk, and to enjoy the cadence of our own polished periods, we are failures. It takes a man of God to preach the word of God. It demands a passion for souls, a great sorrow at the ills of mankind, and a burning consecration to the task of bringing Christ back into this world around us.

How to find out exactly what this particular locality needs is not easy, but it can be done. Know your people, and find out what they are thinking, and make your entrance from there. For example, it was natural to use the barbarism of Buchenwald or any of the Nazi camps as an illustration of what can happen in a world without God; our people could see that, because some of them had existed under that barbarism. Similarly we talk about 'love' when instructing a couple for marriage, because that term and that concept is certainly a common one in modern life; we use that approach to the dogmatic and moral teaching we are going to give, instead of rushing into a logical, but unreal, demonstration of textbook arguments about the Sacrament of Matrimony. Instead of decrying divorce, we try to show that it means the death of that love which these two young people experience so vividly at this moment, and which they are about to consecrate before God. These are little things, but they change religion into a personal, important, even dominant, part of a person's life.

What is your opinion of the 'Sermon Series' which some parishes or Dioceses establish as the programme for a whole year of preaching?

Some sort of planning is necessary, certainly, but it is very important to see that the programme is not a waste of time. It sounds logical, and it is logical, to treat the Creed one year, the Commandments the next year, and the Sacraments during the following year. It is logical, we repeat—but that does not necessarily mean that it is a wise procedure. Life does not run along according to strict *a priori* regulations. Some points in such a programme as the one above demand full treatment here and scanty mention there; this year sees the disappearance of what was an important problem last year. Consequently a ready-made plan has its drawbacks.

Here at Colombes we priests discuss and decide on a year's general subject matter; the decision is made more according to the needs as we see them than according to good order. The first year here we had a general aim of making the faithful conscious of the necessity and possibility of 'conquering' the world around them for Christ. So we emphasized the personal apostolate during October, shifted to a treatment of the Mass, and came back to the meaning of their 'membership' in the church. The over-all theme stayed the same, but the particular treatment varied as we realized the needs and wants of this parish. That same principle held true for all the subsequent preaching programmes, on matters like the family, work, the Sacraments, the Gospels, social doctrine, etc.

Undoubtedly there are plenty of defects and deficiencies in the treatment we give to any or all of these themes. Somehow we would rather be guilty of defects in this attempt to preach the Gospel than to be guilty of the failing which he commits who spends a year preaching against the errors of the Gnostics, or in proving the authenticity of the four Gospels! We would rather commit possible sins of omission in our efforts to stress only the needed doctrines, rather than doggedly and unendingly expatiate on each and every point listed in a year's schedule. Any defect, if defect it be, conforms quite closely to the example of the great Fathers. When Augustine saw Manicheanism and Pelagianism around him, he bore down on those errors; when Athanasius faced Arianism he laid stress on the doctrines which were being attacked. Humbly, but in like manner, we are trying to fit our people to face the two great modern heresies, namely, materialism and Marxism; what is not directly suited for that fight is left reverently to rest in the deposit of Faith. Back in the seminary it was good training to refute Luther and Arius; here in the parish the same refutation is ridiculous—or it would be ridiculous were the times not so critical.

As you admitted earlier in the book, the ones who come to hear us are usually those who are steeped in what you called the 'Parochial atmosphere'. That seems to make your concern about adaptation unnecessary, to say the least.

We did admit that, because it is true. And yet that fact cannot excuse us from trying to adapt the Gospel to modern needs, nor can it permit us to go on with our monotonous clichés. The present dormant state of most parishes is the result of just such an attitude; because we no longer try to

146

awaken our people, they go on in their smug provincialism, their self-satisfaction, their pharisaical formalism. We priests are the cause of all this. Even if there were not millions around us who do not have the Faith, we still are obliged to teach the faithful flock according to the teachings and spirit of Christ. Before we can hope to stir them to a conquest of their pagan neighbours and environment, we must help them rid themselves of all these evil aspects of the so-called 'parochial atmosphere'. Just as some of the strongest words of Christ our Lord were directed against the same parochial self-righteousness, so must ours be.

Sometimes it seems as though we were afraid to tell them the truth. When we do present basic Christian doctrine we take great pains to assure the congregation that we do not intend to include them in our words; we always mean these truths for the 'others', who are not there to hear us. We go out of our way to increase their already dangerous self-esteem by thanking them endlessly for whatever they may have done, even though what they did may have been nothing exceptional. We thank the Women's Guild for their co-operation, the Scouts for their generous efforts, the Men's Clubs for their fine attendance at Mass. This is not a question of politeness, but of unwarranted praise to a people who need a sense of shame for what is not being done. There is no point in treating adults as though they were children, and yet this is what we are doing by our sugar-coated treatment.

Our Lord asked the rhetorical question about what can be used to savour salt that has lost its savour. Claudel's sad reply to this was 'with sugar'. Our sermons and our general attitude would seem to make his answer reasonable. We are not virile enough; even our congregation realizes this. When they try to serve God they know that they are far from perfect; yet, because we constantly laud their efforts and everlastingly hold them up as models for those 'outside', they begin to think that they must be better than their consciences tell them. And so they rest, and preen their feathers, thanks to our own lack of vision. They need a change, and we must be capable of giving it to them.

When a parish has a mission, some of that blindness is corrected.

147

Not necessarily. When you talk about a mission we presume that you mean the occasion when special priests come in for two or three weeks to hold a series of conferences for the men, the women and the children. Such an effort does not infallibly guarantee results, because the times have changed since missions were first begun by St Vincent de Paul and others. In the old days, even up to the turn of this century, missions attracted people who seriously wanted to examine their conscience, or people who realized that they had been doing wrong, and wanted to check themselves. The Faith was there, even when morals were bad; the spark could be easily rekindled. Nowadays missions draw only those who are already Christian; the mass of our population is unaffected despite our efforts at publicity.

Consequently our times demand a change in technique. The notification from the pulpit or by leaflets that a mission is going to be held at such-and-such a time must be reinforced by house-to-house invitations. The talks in church must be replaced by talks in the parish hall or school, because the people we want to attract are really unwilling to enter the church. The subject-matter must change from the traditional Four Last Things to a treatment of doctrine which is especially apt and appealing to this particular neighbourhood. We would even go a little further, and express some ideas of our own on this subject of missions. It seems to us that they would be a great deal more useful if laymen and women were a part of the mission-band, as the Company of St Paul is in Italy. Instead of two weeks they would spend months or years in one locality; they would cover less ground, but they would cover it more effectively. When it came time to leave a section there would be a renewed and growing community behind them, and that includes the parish clergy. Some sections of the diocese might be left neglected, but the ones on whom an all-out effort was concentrated would soon be able to make up the loss to their uncared-for brothers. It seems more practical to emphasize the apostolic work in definite parts of the diocese, and so produce real and lasting good, rather than to spread the labour and the labourers so thinly as to effect no permanent results.

Would you put down for us your conclusions on this chapter?

Certainly. We hold that all the traditional tactics of the Church are, of course, sound, but that they need revision. Missions must be publicized and conducted somewhat along the lines we mentioned, although we do not pretend to utter the last word about this. The congregations which regularly preach missions must discover again the purpose for which they were founded; they must think of themselves as apostles, with a special apostolate, and not merely as secondary aids of the parish clergy. We parish priests must make a special and intelligent effort to bring our preaching into line with the preoccupations of our people. To do that we shall have to strip off the usual coating of clerical culture which covers our words and thoughts, and which renders them unintelligible to the ordinary man and woman of the present century. The principle underlying much of our activity here at Colombes is that we can best reach the minds of our listeners by appealing to their senses. The reader will see in this nothing but a restatement of an old scholastic maxim. Consequently our sermons and services leave room for participation by the congregation, by hymns, processions and similar activity, as was developed in the section on Liturgy.

In whatever we do we try, little by little, to reach the mind and heart of the average man, and to bring him to Christ. Since our background proves to be an obstacle, we do our best to change; since our expression is unsuited, we work to correct it. All of this involves trial and error, and we know that we have made, and will continue to make, many mistakes; but we are trying. Convinced that we have been ordained for the people, and for no other reason, we work as a team with the parish, so that all of us together may best reflect Christ in a world that needs him so badly.

VII THE EQUIPMENT OF MODERN APOSTLES

1. A REAL AND PRIESTLY SPIRITUALITY

Your views are interesting and appealing, but there still remains the difficulty of finding men who can put them into practice.

That is our whole trouble. That lament is made by everybody with whom we have discussed the problems and exigencies of the latter day apostolate, whether they be priests or lay-people. Fundamentally it is not so much a matter of having good methods as of having good men to apply and use them. More important than any other qualification for the priesthood is the apostolic spirit, the alert zeal which a man brings to his people, and by which he can hope to transform them. To paraphrase St Paul's words in the thirteenth chapter of First Corinthians, neither intellectual nor artistic abilities will suffice, although they do help.

You are simply restating the maxim we heard so often in the seminary: 'Be saints, and you will be successful priests'.

We are, but we want to point out that this saying is a much misunderstood one. There are saints and saints. Sanctity is practically as varied in its forms as are the individuals who possess it, because gift differs from gift, and calling from calling. What we are leading up to is this: since we priests have been called to a particular apostolate we hold that this same apostolate must determine and create our particular spirituality. This life is our path to God, and so we must fit and form ourselves to the holiness which this life both supplies and demands. Hence we feel that the proverb you quoted needs explaining, not because we feel qualified to speak as masters of spirituality, nor because we aspire to be the founders of a new spiritual school. We are simply telling you the conclusions we have reached.

As far as we can see, not all types of sanctity are useful for an apostolate to the modern pagan; in fact, some are positive drawbacks. As we go along we shall try to explain all this in our development of two principles:

1. That the apostolate demands an interior life capable of developing a priestly spirituality, properly so called.

2. That the apostolate itself is our proper means of sanctification.

What connection are you trying to establish between the apostolate and our spiritual life?

A necessary one, as you shall see. A little while ago, when we were writing about that thing so close to our hearts, the direct apostolate, we said that priests must share the richness of Jesus Christ with souls who know him not; that the love inside us must spread to all who come in contact with us. You may call that a truism and tell us that the same purpose has been the fundamental reason for all the Church activities of the last fifty years, and we should agree, with qualifications. That purpose was there, but it took an apostle of unusual personal attraction to make the system fulfil its goal; for most priests material concerns connected with the activities killed zeal and obscured the original end.

Almost the same thing has happened to our doctrine. Paradoxically we have learned a great deal about the Trinity, the Incarnation, the Redemption, and but comparatively little about Christ. In the section on preaching we tried to show that we have become better at handling abstract ideas in scholastic form than we have at delivering the message; in our hands Christ has become less of a living Friend and Saviour than the Gospels show him to be. At this point someone will certainly accuse us of belittling the Sacred Sciences, so permit us to explain. We are not saying, nor even hinting, that our years of philosophy and theology were wasted ones, because we unequivocally believe in the necessity of a firm intellectual basis for anyone trying to bring the Truth to this error-ridden world. What we do say is that these abstractions of the schools tend to chill our fervour and check our enthusiasm; it is simply a matter of finding how to put a greater stress on emotional conviction than is now done.

Similarly, spirituality has been affected. Our background tends to make our union with God a stiff and formal thing; we make it a part of our day, but not a part of our lives. Because it is a ready-made affair we find it that much harder to correlate with our attempts to bring others into union with him.

151

When a young man enters the seminary he dreams of conquering the world for Christ; when ordination comes he is less idealistic, but he is still unswerving in his ambition to be a real priest. He comes to his first parish with ideas and ideals, burning with the desire to transform this little corner of the vineyard. We, who are here before him and over him, must make sure that this enthusiasm does not flag because of us. It will not—and this is our main point—if, as a seminarian, this young priest became convinced that his passion for souls will make him a saint. Convinced of it ourselves, we could never understand the attitude of those who regularly dampen the zeal of new curates, who feel that every young priest must be 'cooled off'. Instead of profiting from their sincere example, we older priests, from a secret sense of shame or from some perversity, do more to eliminate that example.

Even back in the seminary that 'cooling off' process was begun. We remember our superior giving a series of talks on zeal; the main theme of every one of them was that we must be prudent in our exercise of that zeal. Good Lord, what was he afraid of? He should have known that internal defects like pride and self-consciousness would do enough to temper the spirit of even the wildest of us. He should have played upon that ardour so as to have us make the most of the seminary years. He should have warned us about the day when our thirst for souls would grow less keen, and when we would be satisfied with much less than our original dreams demanded. If he had showed us that our love for Christ must grow without limit, simply because of the souls that were to find him through us, we might have learned to lean on our zeal, rather than mistrust it.

In other words, you say that there should be at least as much emphasis on spiritual preparation as there is now on intellectual?

Exactly; the only source of a fruitful ministry is a living and vibrant spirituality. Some seem to think that it depends on a special sort of temperament, especially for the direct apostolate to adults which we have been championing. If they mean a compound of physiological and psychological gifts, fired by a certain natural boldness and poise, we do not agree. True, we have to be bold; but that can be fought for and won in battles with our native timidity, and it need not be innate. We repeat that this is a matter of spirituality, not temperament.

In the concrete this is what we mean. For a priest to set out on door-to-door visits, with no assurance whatsoever of a kindly reception, a serious internal disposition of soul is required. Here at Colombes everyone of us is willing to admit that he would not have the courage to do this sort of thing, except for the teamwork we have established. As proof we shamefacedly tell you that each of us spent the first three years here in every other sort of activity, simply and solely because we were looking for excuses not to have to begin this phase of the apostolate, even after we had agreed upon it. As further proof of our thesis, we know of three young priests who asked permission to spend their vacation working in an almost completely de-Christianized section of the country. They had had no practical experience, but they went to that place and talked about Christ to everyone they met; souls came back to him in remarkable numbers, in spite of the fact that everyone thought they would fail. All that they had was an intense love of God, after the manner and example of St Paul; we should not be astonished that this love infected others. I say that these young priests are fortunate, for they are beginning their priesthood by contact with individual souls, and with the determination to do anything to make Christ known and loved by men. We are the unfortunate ones, we who have grown up to look upon our ministry as a mere round of activity, of things to be organized.

Still another proof is found in what militant lay-apostles have told us about their efforts to win souls for Christ; their simple unaffected stories have brought unsummoned tears to our eyes. We marvel at their faith, their courage, their selflessness, and are ashamed that we, though ordained for that very purpose, should be less eager than they in the cause of Christ. The reason? Simply that they have made their spiritual life a cause and an effect of their convictions and we have not. We lead two lives where they have integrated theirs.

Your view, then, is that there is no opposition between the 'Spiritual' and the 'Apostolic' life?

Precisely. As a matter of fact, we would go further, and declare that there is a necessary connection between them. Those who agree that the apostolate demands deep spirituality should also see that the apostolate itself can promote and sustain the spiritual life.

If we were to believe some authors, there seems to be a fundamental opposition between the two, so much so that any attempt to combine them demands a great skill and greater prudence. The spirituality they write about is a thing apart from the grossness of the world; the seminary's purpose, as they see it, is the frantic building up of a reserve of holiness against the day when we shall have no time for spiritual exercises as we know them in the seminary. Once ordained, may God help us! Then we shall have to try to save what we can of our fund of spiritual strength; we shall have to steal a few moments out of each day's whirl of action in order to find God again. So they say.

Remember this. This sarcasm, if such it be, is not directed against the value of the familiar spiritual exercises. We are objecting only to the narrowness and the inaccuracy of those authors who teach this outlook on life in the priesthood.

We believe that our spiritual life becomes infinitely richer and fuller when we build it upon the touchstone of the active ministry, namely, our passion for souls, our apostolate. Rather than consider prayer as *my* contact with God, as *my* duty towards him, it seems less egotistical and more beneficial to see it under this light; namely, to offer it in the name of all those who are not loving God and who are starving without him. This is an expression of the purpose of my priesthood, and will be acted upon soon after I have said my prayers. The alleged danger in this is supposed to be that some of us will fall into an excess of external zeal, will emphasize too much the active life. Possibly, but looking around at the waste of priestly energy, and at the compromise we have to make now, we are not too concerned about this eventuality. More wings are clipped by prudence, criticism and rationalizing than by any excess of zeal; more young priests are in enforced idleness than in intemperate apostolic activity. We see more sophisticated priests than overzealous ones. There is a great deal more verbiage on sins of commission than there is on sins of omission, and yet the latter are chiefly responsible for the present condition of our people.

We know priests who are good, and even holy, men; and yet these same priests can preserve an astonishing tranquility of conscience even though faced by the vision of thousands of souls who live and die around them without the faintest knowledge of Christ, and even though they themselves have been chosen from among men to bring him to such as these. We are astonished and saddened. We know that these priests are regular in their prayers, that they keep up a daily schedule of religious exercises such as they learned in the seminary. Maybe they are too rigid; they are certainly unreal in their spiritual life.

I find it impossible to believe that a priest's contact with God would weaken his apostolic ardour.

We do, too. It can only be that the type of spirituality we have just criticized does not afford real contact with God; the actions are empty, formalistic routine. Such men think that they have done their duty when they have put in the required time or said the indicated prayers; they cannot pretend to have met God in their prayers. Their duty has been carried out to the last detail, but it profits them nothing, at least as regards the vision of souls separated by ignorance and by sin.

It is sad that a priest can arrive at such a state and still consider himself as a 'good' priest. The problems facing the Church demand the full effort of every priest, and yet this man of personal piety is doing nothing for anyone except himself—if, indeed, he is doing even that. It is ridiculous and dangerous to describe a priest as 'good' simply because he is tidy and punctual and steady; part of the reason for these qualities is that he is too selfish or too blind to be unsettled by the gigantic problems, collective and personal, which he should be trying to solve.

Such a man does not reach this state because of his spiritual life; it is the result of a lack of one, or the possession of a misguided one. The one he has is not spiritual and not

155

priestly; it does not know the meaning of *caritas Christi urget nos*. Somehow we cannot see as an ideal that priestly career which sidesteps the troubles and tales of the people he is supposed to sanctify; some priests do, however. We remember one old parish priest who took it upon himself to give some advice to a deacon just before his ordination; the substance of it was that the priest had reached his present enviable position in charge of a wealthy parish simply because he always was smart enough not to waste time listening to people's woes. One of the seminarians present whispered to me: 'just like St Paul!'

What an ideal! It is nothing but that of a petty official, of a soured civil clerk. Among priests it is almost a blasphemy, for we are supposed to be other Christs, living and teaching his Gospel. Again we say that such an attitude could never have arisen except for the prevalent divorce between the spiritual and the apostolic life we are supposed to lead. It is understandable, though not forgivable, only in a man who does not realize that his sanctification is necessarily bound up with his ministry, that his union with God must come from and return into his work with souls. Please God, priests everywhere will come to think on this.

You did admit that some forms of the apostolate were opposed to the spiritual life.

We did, but they are the forms which are least recognizable as being either apostolic or priestly. They include things like athletics, plays, bazaars, and administrative details; these are, properly, the function of lay-people. Accidentally they may sanctify us on account of the patience and self-denial they involve, but, in themselves, they are a distraction, a dissipation of priestly energy. If the spiritual writers mentioned above had meant only this sort of activity, we would most certainly agree with their conclusions.

On the other hand, the direct apostolate is quite another matter. Its source is a thirst for souls; its practice is a constant occasion for seeing and a constant motive for correcting our own shortcomings. We are stimulated to perfect ourselves precisely because we are obliged to see that our defects are an obstacle to others. A priest may easily become discouraged, doing things that have only a remote connection with his priesthood, such as begging for money, or supervising a play; he is less likely to become so when he spends his days and nights in trying to make our Lord known to men. The confidences he receives, the grace he almost creates in the souls of sinners, these will keep alive the grace that was in him on the morning of his ordination; these are natural steps to the feet of the Master. We all know that long hours in the confessional have made us better priests; we all know that a talk to and with militant lay-Christians has made us realize better the meaning of our priesthood. Our preparation for sermons has showed us what it is to meditate. All of these things make us live in a Godlike atmosphere, and they are perpetual goads to do better and to be better. They may not be the best thing for a life of absolute monastic contemplation, but they are the stuff that makes up the essence of an apostolic life. We can even quote St Thomas in our behalf on this particular point, for he taught that the so-called 'active' life has a close connection with the cloistered one; the reason he gives is that the apostle is handling and distributing the gifts of God, and finding his joy therein, in a way similar to the monk's enjoyment of God. We agree with the Angelic Doctor.

Please explain a little more fully what you mean by saying that the apostolate is a spiritual life in itself, and that it is our fundamental means of sanctification.

Our position is based on the idea that our apostolate is not something extra; for us it is a vocation, a state of life. Consequently we hold that we shall not become holy without fulfilling that state of life; nor conversely shall we fulfil it without becoming holy. With every state in life go graces which enable us to perform its necessary duties, for God, who wills the end, also wills the means. Remember that this vocation is a special one—one demanding every ounce of our love and energy and intelligence. Do not confuse our terms, because we do not mean to leave the impression that the apostolate is similar to a job, as the use of the overworked phase 'state of life' might seem to imply. We are not men who can satisfy the demands of our vocation by putting in a certain number of hours, or by performing a certain routine of activity. We have not taken on a job; we have embraced a life. And that life will take from us all our thoughts and all our passion; it will force us to find problems everywhere; it will make us understand, almost automatically, what could be done for Christ in this place or in that situation. No part of our existence, no corner of our minds or hearts is exempt from this drive to break through the path we have been chosen to make for our Lord. If a mother is absorbed by the cares of her family, so are we for the children of God; if a businessman is constantly planning new programmes, new products, so are we for the things of God. We must try to live what St Paul said in his words about 'whether you eat or drink, or whatever you do . . .'.

A priest who is deeply and completely absorbed in this vision of the City of God has already achieved a deep and lasting spiritual life.

But spiritual writers always include the idea of mortification in any outline of holiness.

And we do, too. A priest who is living his parochial apostolate because of zeal for souls need never worry about the fact that we did not mention mortification; he will see that there was no need to develop the obvious. But for the priest who sees in his ministry only a set routine of duty, we hasten to point out to him that the occasions for self-denial are many and great. We can only wish that spiritual writers would begin to outline the practical and ascetical value of the active ministry.

In general, every virtue demands self-denial from those who would practise it; specifically, and in this life of ours, certain ones are more prominent. We shall try to give a brief picture of some of the outstanding sources of the mortification, whose apparent absence some spiritual theorizers might deplore.

The first is Obedience. Not that abstract, though actual, gift of our wills we made to the bishop on the morning of ordination, but the stark, concrete handing over of one's self to the demands of time and place which this life demands. It requires us to accept, without murmuring, the corner God has given us to evangelize, and to see in it the people who are destined to make saints of us while we are trying

to lead them back to him. There is no room for disillusion-
ment, no time for wishing that we were somewhere else, no
slackening of our fervour because of rebuffs. By the same
token we are not to neglect individuals or groups simply
because their poverty or ignorance or crudeness is distasteful
to us. We have been sent to all, and we must obey.

Connected with this obedience is the spirit in which we
must meet the demands on our time. If we are rigid in
allotting every minute of the day and refuse to alter that
programme, we are failing in the true giving of ourselves.
Unexpected visits and often endless talks are a necessary
part of our lives; instead of letting ourselves be annoyed and
out of sorts, we must learn to accept these things as a routine
part of our apostolate, and use them as such. We have
made a gift of ourselves, and we will not take it back. We
are willing to continue with some activity in the parish,
even though we cannot like it; we are willing to live a life
made up of countless tiny and unimportant events, with
none of the dreamed-of fanfare of our youth. Neither
monotony nor lack of success will cause us to forget why
we are here; nor will they reduce our resistance to the point
where we shall have let ourselves become social workers or
sociologists but not priests. There is an obedience for you.
It never lets us go our own way or force our own ideas,
but asks that every priest should accept the situations, the
needs, the people—the warp and woof of our consecrated
labour.

The second virtue we might mention is Detachment.
Abbé Godin brought out the fullness of this at a talk he
gave to a recollection-day group of Jocist girls. He asked
the girls if they should love the Jocist movement; they cried
out that they should. He asked them if they ought to love
their individual cells, and the same reply came back. Much
to the astonishment of all Abbé Godin told them that they
were wrong, that they should be attached neither to the
Jocists nor their particular part of it; the sole object of their
devotion should be the souls of the workers whom they were
trying to bring to Christ. He analysed their feelings, and
showed that the love of one's own cell was nothing but a
disguised self-love which could hinder the apostolate. He

159

pleaded with them to love souls, and to forget themselves, their group, their organization.

While he was talking we could not help thinking of the parish apostolate, and of the application of this great priest's words to our own work. He made us reflect on whether or not we loved our parish. Should we love our parish and our special activities so much? Not to do so, and to think only of souls requires almost an heroic degree of detachment; it asks us to ignore our own success and prestige while we make the welfare of men our sole concern. A little examination of conscience about this virtue could run along lines like the following: if I loved souls and not my own reputation, the knowledge that some of my parishioners go to neighbouring churches for Mass and devotions would not disturb me; my grief would be much better spent on those who go to no church at all. If I loved souls and not my own little kingdom, the absence of militant apostles who felt a greater need for a day of recollection than for the parochial procession I had organized would not infuriate me; I should rejoice at the greater good done to the cause of Christ. If I loved souls more than my parish, the news of an impending division of the parish territory would not make me feel cheated; I should rather be glad that greater attention could now be paid to the tremendous number of souls already in my care.

The same principle will apply to others, as well as to the poor priests against whom so much of the tirading in this book seems to be directed. Sisters and teachers and all the 'officialdom' of the Church might well check up on their own disinterestedness in the service of Almighty God. I remember years ago, how indignant one nun was when I asked her to arrange a mass meeting of two rival groups; she found it impossible that I should be asking that 'her' girls would be expected to share their plans and assets with the other—and inferior—group. Even when I gently reminded her that we were all working for the same Master, her amazed and hurt expression did not change.

If we would only realize that it matters not who preaches Christ, as long as Christ be preached! St Paul, who said those words, could scarcely approve of our jealous departmentalizing, of the careful respect we must show for the boundaries of another man's field. Until we reach the stage where St Paul would be proud of us we are obstacles to the cause he preached, and a scandal to the faithful.

The temptation to go from Detachment to Poverty is too much for us, so please allow us to say a few words on this too. *Wait a minute! Only religious are expected to keep the vow of poverty.*

We know that, but the spirit of poverty is certainly expected of all Christians. We think that there could be and should be an ideal of priestly poverty as a goal for the secular clergy; it would be a marvellous means of mortification as well, and would be far more meritorious than great fasts or the discipline. Speaking very practically we are convinced that this poverty is an important element of the priestly spirituality we are trying to outline.

Above, in talking of money, we spoke about the people's opinion of our middle-class way of living; without repeating all that here, we do want to emphasize the fact that a lowly standard of life is essential to the apostolate among working-class men and women. That means that we shall have to begin to do without many of the luxuries we now enjoy. A seminarian, or a young priest, would not be appalled at the prospect of living simply, but we older priests are. We might admit that poverty in practice would be beneficial to our work, but we can summon a thousand reasons against any drastic change in our position; we, who are settled in this life of comparative ease, are quick to call upon the virtue of prudence and to counsel, sagely, against being too hasty. Our wisdom and our prudence are sadly in need of guidance.

What is asked for is more than a giving up of material luxuries, because more is demanded of a priest who goes to the working-people. As we said previously, we must give up the cultural, artistic, literary delights of our own lives in so far as they hinder us in the work; that they will hinder us, if not closely controlled, is obvious to anyone who knows the average man and also knows the average priest. Please notice that we are not saying that a priest must completely abandon his hours of intellectual and cultural pleasure.

161

Absolutely not! We do say that he must not carry over those tastes in a ministry devoted to men and women who find such things completely foreign to them. We mean that a priest must be willing to work with the dullest of the grammar-school children as well as with the brightest of the high-school age. He will chat with the most unlearned parishioner as readily as he would with his intellectual equals. He will be ready to spend an evening at a Jocist meeting without letting the noise and slang and confusion weary him—at least, not too much.

Such a priest will not spend his time on those who can appreciate his repartee simply because they do appreciate it. His literary gems will be saved for the proper time, and that does not mean all the time. In brief, we are trying to demonstrate that an apostle who is honestly poor in spirit will try to do everything for the good of his people, and nothing solely for his own satisfaction. There is a thorough, unending gift of one's self! By sanctifying the duties God has given us to do we can come to a total acceptance of his will in our regard.

That sounds more like humility than poverty.

Most virtues resemble one another, but we want to thank you for giving us an occasion to say a little about Humility. Parish work could be a splendid source of that virtue for us, but, unfortunately, it often produces the opposite effect.

In this age of contempt for things sacred we are obliged to stress the grandeur of God's priesthood more than ever before. The subsequent danger is that we begin to transfer the majesty from our spiritual position to ourselves; the dignity of the priesthood and the vanity of the priest are closer than most of us realize. A cure for incipient or full-blown pride is contact with ordinary men and women, those who know nothing about the sublimity of the sacerdotal state, and who care less. The ignorance and consequent offhandedness of these people are a tonic to our overweening self-esteem; whether we like it or not, we have to admit that they are not going to let us lord it over them. Knowing that, we have a broad field for the practice of humility, in accepting rudeness, in being pushed into the background, and in the general lack of regard for us. It will do us good.

162

If we knew how workers despise the pompous and dictatorial air we so often assume, we would fight any such tendencies in ourselves. Rather than speak and act imperiously, we should try to imitate more closely the Son of God, who was misunderstood and scorned by the men he had come to save. When we make a morning meditation on humility, we can be sure that the day ahead of us is going to offer plenty of chances for practising what we prayed; our spirituality is given flesh in every circumstance of our lives. Looking back, we are sincerely regretful that our seminary training did not prepare us better for the daily concrete exercise of a tremendously important missionary virtue. The abstract talks on humility were offset, in real life, by the caste system around us in the seminary, by the emphasis on dignity and dignitaries; the same atmosphere carries over into the priesthood, where pious ideals are so easily buried under the weight of existing conditions. We expect and even desire ecclesiastical honours; sometimes we come perilously close to the pharisaism castigated by Christ himself.

It would be humorous, if it were not so tragic, to see the petty things that cripple our apostolicity. An insulting name or a rebuff or a flippant remark is enough to change us from apostles to angry, uncharitable mortals! What a pity! At the cost of souls we defend our wounded dignity, to the sorrow of the faithful, and the scorn of the infidels. The value of our self-esteem relative to that of the salvation of a non-believer makes our attitude all the more pitiful.

Another help in overcoming ourselves in this matter is a deliberate intention to seek and accept the criticisms of parishioners. We are, after all, here for them not for ourselves; and they can see much more and much better than we. Somebody told us about one of the Cardinals of France who asked a Jocist what the people in his surroundings thought of him. Naturally the lad was embarrassed, but the Cardinal pressed him; so the young man told him frankly that people thought that the Cardinal was just as smug as most Catholics were. There was no outburst of rage, but a quiet and sincere request to the Jocist to come back every month and report on how the working-class felt about him. That Cardinal was a great man, and a humble one. We, who claim that the position of the Church would be compromised by permitting laymen to offer suggestions might well think of and imitate the example of this prince of the Church. We might also think on the passage in the Gospel where Christ spoke of the pharisees who loved to be called 'master' and to be saluted in the market-place.

There is no profit in trying to find this spirit of constructive criticism in those whom we might call 'priest-worshippers'; it takes no great sense of honesty to realize that not from them shall we receive truly helpful advice. And yet we can be easily tempted into thinking so, and led to the pathetic lengths of the parish priest who produced two thousand signatures as proof to the Archbishop that his proposed transfer was unwise. If we want to be incensed at the altar and away from it, we can be, and we will be; but it is far better for us and for the apostolate if we know how to take fair criticism and use it to advantage. That needs humility and simplicity.

Do you know what the most common reproach levelled against clergymen is?

It is what some like to call 'prudence', even though they actually mean a sweet sort of decorum and aloofness. That mixture of unction, reserve and self-satisfaction has come to characterize—or caricature—the so-called 'ecclesiastical' art and mannerisms and life. That this should be so is a real tragedy, because it is this very attitude of ours which makes us so repellent to souls longing for frankness, for truth. They reject our polite circumlocutions; they want the doctrine of Christ or they want nothing. In any case they do not want our delicateness. We are wrong to give the name of prudence to such a state of mind, for prudence is a strong weapon, whereas we are indecisive and timid. The people and the times demand stouthearted leaders to point out and lead the way to Christ; and to do it in such a way that our contemporaries will find a fullness for the vacuum they now experience. If we do not do this for them, no one else will or can.

The truth of the matter is that most of us retreat to this misnamed prudence simply because we fear rebuffs, simply because we do not want to have our tranquil lives disturbed. A truer spirituality would realize that these rebuffs and this disturbance are an incalculable source of profit to us and to the souls we are supposed to be directing. What is needed is not haste, not foolhardiness, not brute force, but a profound sense of courage, based on the love of God and man. There is so much to be done.

This seems to be a good place to talk about the spirit of teamwork which you have used with such good results.

We would rather develop that idea a little later on; just now we will mention only the part that it can play in our spiritual advancement. Our experience in the priesthood has led us to two conclusion with regard to teamwork. One is that the modern priest is very definitely called to work as part of a team, not as an individual. The other is that seminaries do not lay enough stress on the formation of flexibility in our character. Seminarians still have their Orders held up because they smoke or talk in violation of the rule, but we do not know of any who are so treated for their haughtiness, bad temper or anti-social attitude. And yet we have seen men in the priesthood who were practically useless just because of these qualities; their moral and intellectual endowments were splendid, but no one, priest or layman, could get along with them. Nowadays, perhaps more than ever before, we need the social virtues as an essential part of our priestly character, both because of the type of person we are trying to convert, and also because of the necessity of united action by the clergy.

In any case, we need the 'community' virtues. The efforts we have to make to acquire them, so as to be a productive member of a team, are immensely valuable to our interior life, as mortifications and as steps towards union with God. Adopting another man's ideas at the expense of one's own, dropping a cherished, personal programme so as to support someone else's, takes greatness of soul. It is a very vivid application of St Paul's words about stripping off the old man.

You would condition the whole life of a parish priest, his prayer, virtues, asceticism, by the parochial ministry. What are you going to leave him for his own, his Mass?

True, we do not leave him very much, but it is better so;

there is no reason why any element of his own spiritual life should be foreign to his priesthood in the parish. Even the Mass, that prime source of interior strength, receives a new and valuable quality from his concern for souls. A Mass which is celebrated with devotion and with exactness has an immeasurable apostolic worth, for a priest is never more a priest than when he is offering the Sacrifice. Here we are other Christs, other High Priests, in an obvious way, going to God for our people, and returning from him laden with graces for the parish. When a priest thinks of the Mass as an act of his private devotion, his spirituality is warped— not to mention his dogma. Essentially the Mass is the worship of the whole Church, of the complete Mystical Body of Christ; in it the faithful are joined to the priest in one communal act of adoration through Christ.

Believe it or not, this incident happened only a few weeks ago, and not in the last century. At a clergy conference one of the venerable parish priests summed up his opinion of Dialogue Masses and para-liturgical ideas by saying: 'at least they should let us say our Mass in peace!' Another priest of our acquaintance forbade his curate to allow the thousand children gathered in the church for a Dialogue Mass in honour of the Blessed Sacrament to utter a single audible sound; he was saying the Mass, and he did not relish being distracted or disturbed at his prayers. These things really happen, lest anyone tell us that every priest realizes that the Mass is not merely his own act of devotion.

If, on the other hand, we have a deep and lively sense of being the chosen representatives of the faithful, we shall want and expect the congregation to participate; our celebration of the divine Mysteries will be for them and with them. The richness we are bringing and distributing will make us one with them, and they with us, and all of us one in Christ Jesus. Both our apostolate and our interior life are progressing by leaps and bounds. Paul Claudel imagined the feelings of a priest at the moment of the Offertory in words like these:

> ' 'The Lord is with you, my brothers. I pray you, be with me.
> Here is more than the paten, more than the chalice and the wine;

Here you are, my little ones, held and supported in
my hands.'

If we could say that and feel that, in our own way, what
priests we should be! We could not help but be different
men, and the souls we most want to attract would be drawn
by Christ in us, the whole community would be joined in
prayer to him through us. There would be no more of those
mumbled, twenty-minute scandals, no more of those meaningless and unmeant gestures. Our own souls and the souls
of the people would grow in our common approach to the
likeness of the Lord.

Surely you understand now why we are pleading for a
synthesis of spirituality and life in the apostolate. One
cannot exist without the other. If we had remained sub-
deacons for life we could find sanctification in reciting the
Office and avoiding sin; as it is we are priests, parish priests,
and surely God meant us to find him in the work he has
given us to do. Instead of the false idea which would have
us flee the field of labour for the strengthening of our souls,
we ought to realize that here, in this parish, are the steps
that will lead us to him. The more perfectly we realize and
use this knowledge, the holier we shall be. More and more,
in the seminary and in the ministry, we should use the
apostolate as the starting-point of all our spirituality. Our
fitness for Orders and for a particular parish should be
judged by our zeal for souls, by our love of Christ; and not
as often happens, by our administrative ability and our
ecclesiastical air. We are not ridiculing or discarding the
standard exercises of piety, which are of great value in and
out of the seminary. But we plead and will continue to
plead, for that attitude which sees the demands of the
ministry as our fundamental and effective source of spirituality, and which admits of no opposition between the two.

2. TEAMWORK

*All the structural reforms you have been explaining are certainly
beyond the strength of even the most courageous priest.*

They are not intended as the work of any one priest, but
of an entire parish team; without that team none of the
ideas proposed in this book can be accomplished. The word

'team' is not satisfactory because we mean so much more than that word implies. We have in mind something more than mere co-operation and co-ordination of the activity of the priests, because the attainable ideal here is a union of the clergy and the people in a single, concerted and militant warfare for Christ. No one is to be neglected, no one is to be outside the group action.

The key to this plan is, naturally, the unity of the parish clergy; unless they are a bloc, it is silly to expect a more complex union with the faithful. If we priests here in this parish had not been closely knit together, what we have accomplished would have been absolutely unattainable; what each has done, all have done. Because of that we can face future difficulties with confidence, trusting in the co-operation we knew in the past to see us through the days ahead. This is not boasting, believe me.

In our times the task we face is so overwhelming that we cannot conceive of anyone trying to face it alone. Without stretching the imagination too far the onslaught of modern paganism can be compared to the invasion of France by the German Army in 1940; our enemy is even stronger, swifter, and infinitely more aggressive. Just as it would have been the height of stupidity to oppose the Nazi army by local and unorganized opposition, so is it more stupid and more costly for us in this latter day. We need an organized counter-offensive which will use every weapon and every Christian according to a long-range and universal plan of attack. Without that we are beaten at the start because of our scattered strength, and because of the delusions of victory which most certainly arise from success in isolated sectors. In the rest of this chapter we shall try to explain the concrete details of our proposal, without any further dependence on military metaphors.

At the beginning of a project like this we need expect no bouquets from anyone, least of all from the average parishioner. They, more than most classes, would rather face death than a change in the life they have always known; the parish may be but half-alive, but this type of parishioner likes it as it is. Love for so-called tradition is equalled only by fear of being disturbed. That is why we had to face the complaints of many an outraged member of our flock, especially in the early days; it took time and firmness and unity on the part of all the priests before the most doubtful Thomases were assured of our good intentions. It was an uphill struggle, and one that never could have succeeded if either the parish priest or the curates had let dissenting parties grow up around them; every denunciation, every criticism, had to be met by the solid unity of all the clergy. In this way not only were meddlers checked, but the enthusiasm of the whole parish team began to be comunicated to the die-hard group.

Under conditions like these a man can work, and work without fear of being considered foolhardy, or of having his ideas discarded peremptorily. The responsibility and errors are everyone's, just as the success is. Failures or mistakes are met with honest but friendly and fraternal correction, and there is no stigma accompanying the errors or the advice. You can see how this makes for peace of soul and strength of effort. Unlike most priests we do not have to face discouragement alone, because we are now bound together in mind and heart and will, in the work of Jesus Christ. Difficulties and criticism are faced together, and 'my work' has become 'our work'.

In this way the isolation that most of us have known in our priesthood is eliminated. We do not have to plan alone, and wonder whether we are right or not; we do not have to be afraid to approach other priests for their ideas. Most important of all, there can be no cleavage between our assigned activity and the advance of the whole parish. Even when things go wrong in our part of the work we are not obliged to face the difficulty alone. The others notice our downcast look, and bring us out of it either by their joking or by their actual help. Before long we really begin to think and act as a team, so much so that we instinctively lean on and support one another.

Even if this solidarity did no more than this, it would be worth while; merely ridding rectories of rivalry and ill-temper is a glorious result. But, over and above this, it touches and transforms our apostolicity with the lighthearted zeal most of us have not known since seminary days. Passing beyond the walls of the rectory, it reaches out to the people, and infects them too. Some readers may smile at this, but one member of the parish actually told one of us that he enjoyed visiting the priests' house, simply because it was such a pleasure to see how well the priests got on with one another. There must be some reason too for the increase of vocations from the parish; and, since we have abolished most of the parish activities, the reason must be found in the evident spiritual joy of the priests. Certainly the words of the Psalmist mean something, and he sang about *quam bonum et quam jucundum*. Nor was Christ joking when he told us that wherever two or three were gathered together in his Name he would be in the midst of them. We live and work, held together 'in the Name of Christ', and that unity is the source of both efficiency and grace for us, and for the whole parish. We know that the faithful notice scandal and discord in their clergy, but we seem to forget that they also notice and imitate our singleminded spirituality.

Could you give us some sort of a definition of this teamwork?

If not a definition we will give you a description. In the first place, it involves *work;* it does not mean simply a common dwelling-place, nor a certain amount of mutual understanding. The team part of it includes all these factors: that the men involved in it are to think the same thoughts, and want the same things; that they better themselves and the work as a unit, by mutual help, correction and compromise.

That is too complicated to grasp. Please explain what you mean by 'wanting the same things'.

We start with the idea that there is to be agreement on certain principles, which are to be the norms for all to follow. This does not say that we lay down a definite programme or method from the beginning; only that all of us agree on the angle from which we are going to face problems as they arise. It is something like fixing a destination before the beginning of a trip. Logically the parish priest should determine these principles, but with the comment and judgement of the curates. They are not to be hard-and-fast rules, because it is almost a certainty that some of them are going to be discarded voluntarily as the work progresses.

In this parish we all did some reading before deciding on the perspective we were to take. If some of Abbé Godin's books had been written then, we might have been spared a lot of reading. Our dinner-table became a round table of ideas; to it we invited priests and laymen who were familiar with the problems and spirit of the working people. Partly for the fun of it, and partly for our own good, we decorated the dining room with placards, on which we printed different slogans. One was Pope Pius XI's 'We think so much of traditions that we do not hesitate to create new ones'. Another was from a letter of Saint Francis de Sales: 'Popes are generally willing to let custom authorize things which would be awkward for the popes themselves to authorize.'

Once the important over-all principles have been agreed upon, it is essential to convince each one of us that our individual efforts and thoughts are needed. We cannot succeed without each other. That must be understood and acted upon in practice. Even when we cannot see eye to eye on particular points, we still realize that the total plan depends on all of us. We used to joke about our 'Five Year Plan', but we knew that each of us would work together, through thick and thin, to see that task fulfilled. We wanted to bring this entire parish back to the feet of Christ. We all wanted that.

When it comes time to decide upon details it takes the goodwill and intelligence of all of us. There is no place for personal goals which would split the team into factions. We have our own particular assignments, but not to the extent of resenting the intrusion of one of the other priests, and not to the extent of believing that we can handle our share of the work without the co-operation of all the priests. It may sound as though we are fond of chaos, but let the reader be reassured. Each man is complete master of his particular task, but he does not have to assert his independence by jealous irritation in order to prove it. He has reached the stage of conviction where he sees himself and his function as part of a bigger and more important whole. We have willed to work together. Essentially, that is what we mean by 'wanting the same things'.

Still, being human, you must encounter difficulties in the practical application of this common will.

We should, if it were not for the fact that we 'think the same thoughts'. We said that both the goodwill and the intelligence of each priest were necessary for the realization of our over-all plan. The curates are not simply the errand boys of the parish priest's preconceived ideas, but they are meant to give themselves totally to the task confronting all of us. In a discussion anyone may raise a question, and all try to answer it; no one is to insist on the correctness of his own view, because then the driving force of the team would vanish. Everyone is to be heard, no matter how rash his views may be, but everyone is expected to be willing to face the opinion and decision of the majority. Once settled, the idea becomes common property, and opposition is put aside, without bitterness by the opponents and without gloating by the defenders. There is plenty of room for differences, but absolutely none for contrariness.

Our experience has been that we grow closer together as we go along; being so close together we think as a community almost by second nature. At the beginning of each week there is a special meeting to decide upon pressing needs, but, for the most part, we find ourselves working and thinking together without adverting to it. Honestly, it has reached the stage where we hesitate, in a sense, to act without consulting our confrères. By this time a parishioner no longer shows surprise when the parish priest says that he wants to talk over the proposal of the parishioner with one of the curates before deciding upon it.

At first glance such an attitude on the part of the priest may seem harmful to good order, to authority and obedience. Somehow it does not work out that way. Everyone realizes that the parish priest has a better general knowledge of the needs and capabilities of the parish, and that his experience in the priesthood is fuller. Quite naturally it devolves upon him to decide the general directives, and his position and experience are enough to settle any discussions which threaten to be interminable. Obedience to him, too, is all the easier because it is free and not forced; it is given to him willingly because of the sacred task of all the priests in the parish. He is not a dictator, but a leader. He himself is bound to obey and submit to the demands which the common good lays upon all. Consequently obedience becomes not a burden but a joy. No one is asked to be a slave, but all are asked to make a complete consecration of themselves. Parish priest and curates alike are involved in this, and each is given chances to understand the peculiarities of the other. In our opinion the issue at stake here is infinitely more important than any secondary considerations, and our first concern must be to ensure the basic need, namely, the transformation of our parish by the co-operation of all its members.

Another result of excessive preoccupation about authority and obedience is that it may well prevent a curate from speaking his mind when he should do so. This is especially true of a newcomer, who will fail to catch the spirit of the team and will get the idea that he is neither wanted nor needed unless he is made to understand that he will not be treated as a child when he does speak out. His opinions must not be met with sarcasm or mere indulgence. It is the privilege of the young to make mistakes, precisely because they are young and visionary and enthusiastic. We need that vision. If the emphasis is placed on authority, the teamwork comes to a full stop; instead of developing and building apostles, we shall have discouraged and cynical priests on our hands. That is no pleasant prospect.

It is easy enough to think along the same lines, but it must be much more complicated when each one takes up his assigned work.

It is, but our convictions and principles remain the same. Even though each of us has a definite assignment we still act as a unit. You see, we think of what we are doing as *the* work, and not *my* work, even to the logical conclusion that none of us feels free to take time off, as long as one of us has something to finish. But since we are men, not angels, we have to take precautions against hurting one another's feelings, because common sense and bitter experience have proved sensitiveness to be the number one enemy of teamwork. This means that it is difficult to divide up the work; it prevents a man who spots an oversight in someone else's plans from correcting the mistake. However, if we have to watch our every word with one another for fear of giving offence, if we have to wonder and worry about the reaction of the others, we might as well forget about co-operation. Unless we know for certain that each of the others will not object to what we do in good faith, unless we are sure that all the others think and will as we do, our labour is in vain; we are not a team. We are no longer striving for the advance of the Kingdom of God in this parish, but for our own reputation or satisfaction.

All of this involves sacrifices. The end in view is so important that sometimes we have to curtail some particular phase of it for the good of the whole; such a decision has to be taken graciously by the priest affected. Murmuring or insinuation or becoming a martyr can ruin the spirit and the very existence of our common work. When a man can take such reversals in his own field of endeavour, he is practising a most profound mortification—one of inestimable benefit to himself and to our work. Such a man is well on the way to conquest of self, and he has found the real meaning of obedience.

Tell me, what is the meaning of the charts and graphs in your rectory?

They are there as proof of the advances and the failures of our teamwork. Once a week we have a meeting to discuss the past week's accomplishments; the results are traced out on these graphs, which show the picture of five years of effort. We comment on the findings, on the attendance at services, on our sermons, etc. No one is spared, not even the parish priest. It is easy to see the advantages of such a system. For one thing, it guards against routine; every one of us is stimulated and corrected, whereas we should almost certainly become dangerously self-satisfied if left to our own tender goading. Everyone has a chance to speak aloud the words that we should otherwise say behind one another's back, to the loss of charity and to the detriment of our work.

Do not imagine, though, that these meetings are completely negative. Besides the failures, there are also the individual and common successes to be talked over, with encouragement and renewed fervour for all. That is equally important. But the chief value of such meetings is the concentration of many single-minded hearts and wills on problems common to us all. Where, alone, we might have been satisfied with a vague uneasiness that something was wrong, here, in the bonds of charity, we try to find out just where we have gone wrong, and then put it right. Two heads are better than one, and we proceed accordingly. We try to use to good advantage that deeply rooted tendency of man which makes him see the mote in his brother's eye before the beam in his own. Everything that we do is fair prey for this criticism, and we are better men and better apostles for it.

Most young curates are agreeably surprised when they find such a system. It relieves them of that dread of doing the wrong thing and not being told about it, for new curates can find themselves in very awkward positions simply because no one told them about their mistakes. We try to ensure against both the mistakes and the anxiety, while the good-natured spirit of the meeting forestalls even the trace of a persecution-complex. Moreover, the newcomer does not have to face the jaundiced barbs or the paternal condescension of individuals; this is a mutual task of like-minded men.

What parishioners say about us comes up for discussion too, and this is especially valuable, since it shows the reactions of the very ones we are trying to influence. Without these meetings and this team-work the value of parish reaction and comment would be lost, for it would take a rash man indeed to tell a confrère in private what the parishioners are saying about him! As it is now, the comments can be revealed, since we take them as applying to all of us.

We are personal too. We are ready to discuss our ministerial work, our temperament, character and deportment. Every year, just before the annual retreat, we take advantage of the spiritual mood which comes upon us, and gather around for an old-fashioned chapter of faults. Each of us, in turn, is sent out of the room while the others pick out traits to be conquered or developed by the one in question; as he leaves for Retreat the next morning, he is handed a sealed envelope, to be used during the week as food for examination and meditation, by a chastened retreatant.

This includes the parish priest. In this way we actually do help one another; the steps along the way to our perfection as priests and missioners are marked out for us. Each of us knows in his heart that all the others are with him, that their criticisms are sincere and unmistakable manifestations of love and support.

What did you mean in your definition of team-work when you spoke about compromising oneself?

Maybe an example will show what we mean, because an abstract explanation is extremely difficult.

Supposing a parishioner approaches a curate with a complaint about the parish priest. For the sake of example, let us even suppose that the parish priest might very probably be wrong in this particular matter. Now three possibilities are open to the poor curate. He may condemn his superior and justify the parishioner, which seems unwise, to say the least. Or he may listen patiently to the long explanation, try to illuminate the reasons for the parish priest's decision, while keeping himself completely out of the argument. Or he may refuse to accept any rebellion, any swerving from the decision made by the parish priest, in such a way that the parishioner cannot help but see that the curate identifies himself with the decision.

At first glance that last possibility may seem to be sheer stubbornness. At second glance it may still seem stubbornness; however, we hold that, taking things as they are, a parish team must follow such an attitude wholeheartedly and unswervingly. We know that complaints are going to come, and we must prove to the opposition that we are a solid and convinced bloc; once we let the wedge of individual adherents enter into our common life as priests, our co-operation is lessened or lost. There must be no little group round Father So-and-so, no devotees of Father Such-and-such— at least, not to the extent of putting a particular priest outside the team. After a while people will see that our inflexibility in this matter is meant for their benefit. It asks sacrifices of people and priest, but it is an immensely important part of our programme.

It seems to me that your little community is a happy one, judging from what I observed in the time I spent here.

It is, as a result of another principle of ours, namely, that we enjoy ourselves; when we need relaxation we try to relax together. Basically it is the same idea as that which underlies the granting of holidays in a seminary. When the students show signs of tension a free day makes new men of them. Also, we try to be a little family unto ourselves, and so our jokes and teasing are very much like the ones we all knew in our own homes. It is difficult to describe, just as the humour of any family might well seem strange to an outsider. We have found our own ways of relaxing together and of enjoying one another; any other group can achieve the same in its own way.

You must have a high opinion of community life.

We most certainly do. Not that we confuse it with the religious life, its vows, of Poverty, Chastity and Obedience, its rules and spiritual exercises. Rather, we have in mind a kind of Community life which will be possible for secular priests. Such a community involves a minimum of being together physically, for we hardly see each other in the course of a day; spiritually, though, we are together as much as possible. 'Living together' is nothing else but adapting ourselves to one another, according to the particular and peculiar gifts of temperament, character and grace which are given each of us. The very diversity of these talents is a treasure which we must uncover and use. As a matter of fact, it is a good thing that others are not like us, that they have a different standard of values, see things that escape us, and are rich where we are poor. Even our defects are to be accepted, for they usually are but the excess of our good points, and we can help each other in their correction. Maybe one of us is a little too boisterous and noisy and disrupts the community life a little; maybe he is the type who sings in a loud voice while we are trying to write up a sermon . . . but it is he who makes us rock with laughter when everyone else is gloomy. Perhaps another one of us is a trifle too meticulous and precise, but it is he who keeps order in our accounts and records.

Living together necessarily creates a certain community feeling; just what that will be depends on the individual community. It is made up of this one's speed and that one's slowness; of vision and of solidity; each plays upon the other, until the rhythm is found—like oarsmen in the same boat. The parish priest must temper the rashness and check the exuberance of the quick, and make sure that the less dynamic are appreciated.

Does this community life extend to the supernatural sphere?

Indeed it does, for we are not merely propagandists; we are also and especially priests—members of Christ, the High Priest, intermediaries between God and man, appointed to bring the divine Life to men. A vocation such as this is a stronger reason for mutual support and collaboration than is the mere organization of apostolic tactics. We must be a team in the supernatural sphere, so as to climb together, and so as to raise the spiritual level of the whole group. We must give the best that is in us, as God has given to each, and try to profit from the best that is in everyone else. We must pray together, not by any scheduled 'exercises', even when that would be possible, but by a union of hearts in prayer.

Take the question of prayer. A necessary preparation for it is this very state of being united. Its first requisite is that the charity of Christ be spread among us, raising our hearts to the Father. If we were to examine our distractions at prayer, we should find that many of them are caused by bitterness and rankling left from some little quarrel. In a community which is not united we could say that most distractions come from difficulties in adapting ourselves, from 'fraternal' collisions; the greater part of our spiritual forces is expended on defending charity against these on-slaughts. If we were united our prayers would, at least, be free of this care. So much for the negative side. Positively speaking, if we were each as greatly concerned over the spiritual level of the whole team as we are over our own spiritual progress, if we were anxious to open up and give of our best to the others, we should not hesitate to express our personal opinions about prayer, or about the little helps that we have discovered. This is a difficult thing to do, and consequently it is rarely done. We are ready enough to exchange views on an intellectual plane; it is only with real friends that we can exchange experiences on what we feel down inside us. Yet something like this must be reached in our priestly teams, because priests who live the same supernatural and priestly life should be friends. We cannot be bashful if we want this teamwork to succeed, but we must be willing to express ourselves without waiting for somebody else to begin.

Why not have spiritual reading in common? Not the formal kind, when the parish priest imposes a book of his choice on everyone, but the spontaneous type, where a member of the team reads a passage that caught his fancy. Even better, there could be a subject proposed for everyone to discuss and where everyone can read what he found of interest or of value on the subject. That is how we often do it at Colombes. The result is far richer than would be obtained from listening to one man's ideas.

The same is true of all spiritual exercises. If we keep watch before the Blessed Sacrament, it is in the name of all; if there is a parochial offensive under way, all are joined in prayer before the Tabernacle. When we recite our Breviaries, it is spiritually 'in choir', for all of us are ordained for the praising of God. When we celebrate Mass, we 'con-celebrate' in spirit with all those whose task and privilege it is to offer the Sacrifice of Christ in the name of and for the benefit of the parish. Even though, canonically, the Mass *pro populo* binds only the parish priest, we celebrate it every day, as a share of all the Masses offered by all the priests of the world. When one of us has some special difficulty, it is natural and easy to get another one of us to meet for prayer with him.

This common prayer is a great boon to us. It is—as it must be—really fraternal, and really in harmony with our lives.

This life as a team certainly must be a tremendous source of strength. But it must also involve a considerable degree of mutual consideration.

It does: Living as a unit is a good purifying agent, to use the terms of spiritual writers. It involves detachment, submission to the trials of daily life, a constant struggle against pride and jealousy. We have to forget the 'ego', give up many

179

of our own little likes, value the good opinion of others, and accept the others, so as to catch the rhythm of the team. There is a crying need for simplicity, but you know as well as we how difficult it is to attain it. And yet, once we have begun the struggle to make it a part of our lives, a new peace and a new joy are ours; the interior and the apostolic life are enriched and increased. It involves mortification, but the type of mortification which is proper to our priestly lives, and it eliminates other unnecessary or incompatible ascetic approaches.

From conversations or letters we know for a fact that many young priests would like to unite with their fellow curates and with their superior in this sort of team. It could be done, more easily than many believe; we sincerely hope that it will be. As conditions are now, diocesan authorities seem more preoccupied with particular local needs than with the possibility of assigning priests to rectories where they might find men who would be both willing and able to work as a team. We are not being critical, but we do long for the day when a long-range vision will inspire the appointments of the clergy; and we pray for the day when a priest will be sent to a certain place, not because the parish priest needs another curate, but because this particular priest will fit well there.

What advice could you give to a newly-formed team?

Our first advice, if such it is, would be to have each man firm in his determination to make the union of minds and wills work, even though other members of the team may be slow in forming the necessary attitude.

Coupled with this must be what might be called 'perpetual motion'. By that we mean a ceaseless fight against slipping into a routine; a new routine, to be sure, but one that can solidify as quickly as the old one did. We must have the same revolutionary spirit that led us to come together as a team, and the first fervour and freshness must be maintained by a healthy dissatisfaction with the results that we have obtained and by a continual seeking for new outlets. It is not enough to have a few novel ideas at the beginning and then to sink back into lethargy and routine; for the existence and for the fruitfulness of our work there must be unending adaptation to the changing problems of our ministry.

You mentioned getting the whole parish into this team. How do you go about that?

The priestly team must be no more than the nucleus of the parochial one. The latter could not exist without the previous priestly formation; but this, in turn, must include all the active elements of the parish from every corner of it.

After all, why not get the parish interested in its own welfare? When we talk about a parish we certainly mean the people more than the priests; they were here before we were, and will, no doubt, be here long after we have been sent to some other post. We are no more than go-betweens for them, and so should get rid of the mental confusion which makes some parish priests say 'I am the parish'.

What a pity, when the faithful confuse the parish with the priests who direct it. Because of this attitude they no longer think that it is their affair too, and that they ought to be interested in it.

It will always be difficult for some to join in any united effort. Many priests, realizing this, ask no more than that the faithful should do what they outline for them. We say that this is not the way to form virile, stalwart characters which the Church needs so badly.

To join priests and people in one team means more than simply calling meetings and setting up committees with no more results than a vague feeling of accomplishment. We must so act towards our people that they may be really and completely united to the life and progress of their parish.

We have lay-movements; let lay-people take charge of them! Let them realize that this is *their* movement, and that they do not have to be constantly worrying about what the parish priest will think; outside of questions of faith, morals, or things touching the welfare of the entire parish, they themselves should be capable judges. We must leave them alone in their organizing, in their formation, so that they can acquire a necessary sense of responsibility. When they are needed for some development within the parish they should be treated as adults, not children. They should be asked to help, and given reasons why they should; they should be allowed to see the end in view, and not be asked to follow our commands blindly. Especially should they be encouraged to speak to us, spontaneously, about their ideas and desires and grievances, and to let us know the criticisms which occur to them or to their neighbours.

More than one splendid suggestion has come to us in this way at meetings of militants. We should get them used to feeling free to speak to us, without fear or flattery. They ought to know that we are sufficiently mature not to resent reproaches; they ought to be able to see that we can tolerate their holding an opinion contrary to our own, without our claiming that they have insulted our priestly dignity.

Every member of the parish, whether he or she belongs to any of the specialized movements or not, should feel wanted and useful. More commonly in our parishes the whole burden of any apostolic attempts that may be made falls on a few 'directors'; everyone else accepts this fact, and even welcomes it. The truth is that for any movement the great majority of people are 'followers'. That we realize. However, we want to see *everyone* progressively more and more interested, personally, in the advance of the cause. Nothing more harmful to such progression could be conceived than the custom, as it prevails in too many parishes, of having periodic meetings of these 'directors', so that the parish priest can give to them tasks that he has drawn up for them. They are changed into agents, whereas they are meant to be leaders. Imagine for yourselves how a Jocist group would feel if the leader were to present them with a set of ready-made objectives, which he had dreamt up, and which they must somehow harmonize with the purpose of the group. Surely there are better ways to awaken and sustain the zeal of our people!

One better way is to outline the task and objectives to the whole body of the faithful when they are present at Sunday Mass; then they can feel their unity and participation. From that same pulpit we can give them an up-to-date outline of the work of the whole parish, of failures, successes, mistakes and advances, and of things yet to be done by all of us. Sometimes the best sermon that a parish priest could preach is precisely this sort of outline.

Since the parish is not only a place of activity, but also a family, it follows that the parish priest should be a father, and that his simple speech and evident sincerity should be directed to training his children to react properly to the demands of the family's common goal.

It is essential that this spirit of generosity and vision enter into every single heart and join it to every other member of the parish, so that all may grow to full stature in this mission atmosphere.

VIII   A GLANCE AT RESULTS

The logical question now is: Do your ideas and methods produce results?

That question is a perennial one, but not necessarily logical. After all, spiritual realities cannot be measured by a slide-rule, nor should proof be demanded to determine the value of apostolic efforts. Results, in the kind of work we are doing, may be barely visible, but God alone is the competent judge of the worth of our efforts. What is begun with a great fanfare may easily end in silence; and what begins quietly and perhaps inauspiciously can just as easily grow and be successful. God gives such increase. It is almost impossible for anyone to foresee all the factors which are going to play upon any particular missionary scheme; and the men and women involved in it, the political and social trends surrounding it, all have an influence upon its apparent success or failure. In work like this it is practically impossible to judge results fairly and accurately. Even while we use statistics and charts (as we do), you know as well as we that statistics can prove almost anything. Even when people begin to acclaim any particular activity as 'remarkable', 'eminently successful', we still do not have any proof that the results they acclaim are being accomplished. God knows, and we would rather trust in him than in mathematics or publicity.

The figures that we have kept show a steady, unspectacular growth over the last five years, and we will put them down here for whatever they may be worth.

Attendance at Sunday Mass was as follows:

1941—1,000 (average)   1944—1,100 (Evacuation of
1942—1,100   Paris)
1943—1,200   1945—1,300

Attendance at the Easter Retreats is more encouraging:

	Boys	Girls	Adults		Boys	Girls	Adults
1941 ..	75	80	135	1944 ..	85	135	230
1942 ..	70	90	150	1945 ..	135	165	230
1943 ..	100	100	170				

In a large parish like this it is extremely difficult to compute the number of those who made their Easter duty. As far as we could determine, these are the figures:

1941	..	850	1944	..	1,250
1942	..	930	1945	..	1,375
1943	..	1,070			

A rough estimate of daily Communions shows that, in 1941, there were 19,000 Hosts distributed; in 1945 the number had grown to 42,000.

We put down these records without trying to deceive ourselves or you about their value; all that they prove is that we have a great deal of work yet to do. Over these last five years we have won a considerable amount of sympathy and interest, but we certainly have not changed much of the pagan atmosphere around us. We have begun, though, and the attendance of non-believers at para-liturgical or simplified ceremonies is frequent enough to make us believe that the beginning is a good one.

Could you give us any estimate of the converts you have made?

The majority of those whom we have received into the Church are lapsed Catholics, whom the grace of Lent or a mission has brought back to the fold. Besides these there are some new adult converts every year, but the number is small, and the obstacles to their perseverance are great. As Abbé Godin pointed out, the modern parish has practically no influence on the mass of irreligious or indifferent persons inside its territory. That truth partly explains the scarcity of conversions, and it also leads us to the two conclusions that:

The Mission of Paris is a strict necessity;

Parishes must aim at the conversion and at the perseverance of non-Catholics.

Consequently it is not enough to make a parish missionary-minded and then to consider the battle won; we need every possible means of evangelization that we can lay our hands on to supplement and support the over-all effort of a mission-parish. All that we have written in this book about the gulf between clerical and popular mentalities, about the 'collective' mentality of modern man, is meant to drive home the lesson that we must bombard and overpower non-believers by the very ceaselessness and diffusion of our efforts. We need men with ideas and with courage to pioneer where the rest of us may be able to follow; and we, who lack the vision and the strength to vary from the traditional paths, should give thanks to God for raising up such men in these times. *Dummodo Christus annuntietur!* When love of God and zeal for souls are the occasion of a man's mistakes, we should do better to imitate him than to laugh at him.

THE RECEPTION OF CONVERTS

Why is the perseverance of adult converts such a serious problem?
There are many reasons; sometimes such apparent ones as the fact that a particular conversion was not completely sincere, or was made only to make easy a marriage with a Catholic partner. In any case we are faced with the spectacle of non-Catholics who took instruction, received Baptism and First Communion, and who now are outside the Church; that spectacle is frequent enough to make us want to do something about it. Certainly the power of the Gospel has not waned, nor is Grace lacking to strengthen and confirm converts to the Faith. And yet many fall away.

The principal natural reason for this type of apostasy is found, we think, in the failure of the Christian community to receive and adopt these newcomers. Few of us can stand alone in anything; we are not made that way. Fewer still are the modern persons who can break with their old religious or social group and persevere in that decision, unless their new group immediately and completely absorbs them. Hence we must make special and practical efforts to fill the gap in the lives of recent converts and make them a real part of the new community ourselves. That is why we have written so much about the communal nature of the modern parish, and why we believe so strongly that every parish should be a religious family, with every neighbourhood and street united by the one parish bond. Our times need a community of souls, of interest, of worship.

If the parish to which an adult convert comes can offer him that support, he is no longer alone, no longer isolated both from the community he left and from the community he joined. On the other hand, if his new-found comrades in the Faith are not themselves bound together in interests and worship, he is very likely to drift off again. He was hungry, and we did not take him in.

Making converts a part of our community will, then, guarantee their perseverance?

Not in itself, but it is a very important part of that guarantee, naturally speaking. Above and beyond that, there are certain 'dos' and 'don'ts' which we ought to observe in our welcome of converts. The list that we include here is taken from the recommendations made to us by a young man who was himself recently received into the Church.

1. Most converts go through an intellectual and emotional battle before they enter the Church, and her doctrines and ceremonies are completely new to them. Remember that, and try to understand the enthusiasm and the curiosity they manifest.

2. Realize that the material side of Catholicism, such as collections, stipends, etc., can scandalize the exalted motives of new Catholics. Make allowances for their attitude, and try to reduce the occasions of such scandal to a minimum.

3. External manifestations of religion, such as the Sign of the Cross, genuflections, etc., do not come easily to most converts, because their background was so different from that of lifelong Catholics. Try to put them at their ease.

4. Give a convert some outlets for his new-found zeal. Introduce him to activities or circles suited to his inclinations, and help him to meet Catholics who will edify and sustain him. Remember that 'ordinary' Catholics are going to be a stumbling-block to his ideals.

5. Make him feel wanted and accepted, in every way possible, for he has made a great sacrifice for the great treasure he has won.

All of these points could be enlarged upon, but we have touched upon them often already. It is up to the priests of every parish to apply them according to local needs. We are priests in order to bring Christ to the world and to find the sheep that are lost; the ninety-nine whom we leave behind (even though the modern proportion is considerably less) will understand our preoccupation for the lost members of the flock. They will come to see why our sermons and ceremonies are directed to the outsiders, and they will even come to agree that we should prefer the lost to the found. Before long the faithful will be as mission-minded, as convert-conscious, as we are.

This process works in a circle. The converts we make by our communal effort continually strengthen and enliven the very community that helped to make them Catholics. They are both the fruit and the fuel of the labour of the whole united parish. Provided that we do not enervate them by any foolhardy attempts to 'ecclesiasticize' them, nor repel them by the scandal of our indifference or materialism, these converts are the greatest source of energy that any parish can hope to have. They are the new shoots grafted on the old vine, and we can well use that new life.

CONCLUSION

At the beginning of this book we resolved not to paint the picture of our work here as though it were a masterpiece and a model; now that we have reached the end, we cannot help but wonder how well that resolve was kept. Poorly or well, we still mean it. The examples and details given here are not intended for reproduction, because, for the most part, they belong only to this setting. Our hope is that no one will make that mistake. Our intention was, and is, to stimulate the missionary apostolate, and not to praise our own version of it.

Let each parish strive to make its liturgy splendid and full of meaning. Let each parish make of itself a real community, devoted to the conquest of souls, and united within itself for that single goal. Let every parish priest avoid the pitfalls of money, of 'clerical culture', of remoteness from the thoughts and needs of his people. Let all, priests and people, be anxious to find new ways of bringing Christ to those who do not know him, and capable of following those new paths. That is our message. In giving it we could not help but localize our realization of it, but we did not mean to limit it to our abilities or to our results.

If anything that we said seems revolutionary or wild-eyed, it was not meant as such, and, in reality, it is not. Our inspiration was from the Gospel, in which all may see that Christ meant us to be united, meant us to make him known to our fellow-man, and meant priests to be priests, not clerks, nor organizers, nor officials. Péguy described a revolution as an appeal from a less perfect tradition to a more perfect one. Because we agree so heartily with him, this book came to be written.

May it be an inspiration for a rebirth of apostolic zeal!